Combining Service and Learning in Higher Education

Evaluation of the Learn and Serve America, Higher Education Program

Maryann J. Gray
Elizabeth H. Ondaatje
Ronald Fricker
Sandra Geschwind
Charles A. Goldman
Tessa Kaganoff
Abby Robyn
Melora Sundt
Lori Vogelgesang
Stephen P. Klein

with

Nancy Campbell
Kathy Rosenblatt

RAND Education

RAND

The research described in this report was supported by the Corporation for National and Community Service.

ISBN: 0-8330-2725-5

Building on more than 25 years of research and evaluation work, RAND Education has as its mission the improvement of educational policy and practice in formal and informal settings from early childhood on. RAND is a nonprofit institution that helps improve policy and decisionmaking through research and analysis. RAND® is a registered trademark. RAND's publications do not necessarily reflect the opinions or policies of its research sponsors.

Published 1999 by RAND
1700 Main Street, P.O. Box 2138, Santa Monica, CA 90407-2138
1333 H St., N.W., Washington, D.C. 20005-4707
RAND URL: http://www.rand.org/
To order RAND documents or to obtain additional information, contact Distribution Services: Telephone: (310) 451-7002; Fax: (310) 451-6915; Internet: order@rand.org

PREFACE

This report presents evaluation results of the Learn and Serve America, Higher Education (LSAHE) initiative, sponsored by the Corporation for National and Community Service (CNS). CNS is an independent federal agency that operates AmeriCorps, the National Senior Service Corps, VISTA, ACTION, and Learn and Serve America, among other programs. Learn and Serve America aims to incorporate community service into academic learning in both K–12 education and higher education.

This report addresses impacts of LSAHE on students, communities, and higher education institutions and is based on three years of data collection and observation conducted by RAND from Fiscal 1995 through Fiscal 1997.

This report serves three audiences. First, the findings offer feedback that can help CNS plan for the future of LSAHE. Second, national policymakers may find the results relevant to decisionmaking about future federal support for LSAHE. Third, higher education administrators and practitioners may find the report useful for program and policy development at the campus level.

CONTENTS

FIGURES

TABLES

SUMMARY

The last decade has seen a substantial increase in efforts by colleges and universities to involve students in community service, particularly a special form of community service known as *service-learning*, which uses service to promote the learning and development of the service provider (i.e., student). Proponents of service-learning believe that it helps students learn more, increases their preparation for and understanding of the responsibilities of living in a democratic society, and addresses pressing social problems facing communities. Hundreds of college and university presidents along with major higher education associations and some highly influential scholars actively support the development and growth of service-learning within the higher education sector. At the same time, others within higher education—especially faculty—are skeptical of the benefits of service-learning, particularly when service is integrated into for-credit academic courses (called course-based service-learning). Critics contend that service waters down the curriculum, further weakening the quality of higher education, and that the time students spend volunteering in community agencies as part of a course might be better spent in the library or laboratory. To date, research on service-learning has yet to resolve fundamental questions about its impacts on either students or communities.

OVERVIEW OF LSAHE

The Corporation for National and Community Service (CNS), established by the National and Community Service Trust Act of 1993, is among the supporters of service-learning. Its initiative called *Learn and Serve America, Higher Education* (LSAHE) is designed to nurture the development of postsecondary service-learning programs. LSAHE strives to:

- Engage students in meeting the unmet needs of communities;
- Enhance students' academic learning, their sense of social responsibility, and their civic skills through service-learning;
- Increase the number, quality, and sustainability of opportunities for students to serve.

To achieve these goals, CNS awards grants to higher education institutions and a small number of community organizations for the development, expansion, or enhancement of courses or programs that involve students in service as part of their education. From Fiscal 1995, the first year of operation for LSAHE, through Fiscal 1997, CNS awarded about $10 million to approximately 100 grantees each year.

These grantees included some *single institutions* and some *consortia*, or groups of institutions linked to a central hub. The consortia hubs used their LSAHE grants to award subgrants to member institutions, a small number of which then awarded subsubgrants.

Through subgranting, LSAHE funds reached between 365 and 458 higher education institutions nationwide each year.

Grant recipients generally used their funds to support a variety of service-learning courses and extracurricular programs. LSAHE funds were typically combined with other sources of support for service-learning and used to seed a number of service initiatives throughout the campus. For example, many grantees used their funds to support service centers that coordinated a wide variety of service activities. Others provided release time or incentive grants to faculty to develop new service-learning courses, in efforts to infuse service into the curriculum.

Regardless of whether service-learning was provided through courses or co-curricular programs, LSAHE encompassed two broad types of activities: direct service and capacity building.

- *Direct service* activities were intended to engage students in meeting community needs and promote student learning. LSAHE-supported staff and faculty placed, trained, supervised, and monitored student volunteers, coordinated service programs, and taught service-learning courses. About four out of every five LSAHE grantees engaged in direct service. CNS encouraged the development of service programs in four areas: education, health and human needs, the environment, and public safety.
- *Capacity building* activities were intended to strengthen institutional support for service-learning and increase the number, variety, and quality of service opportunities for students. These activities included designing courses, establishing databases of service opportunities, providing workshops for faculty about service-learning, helping others develop service-learning programs, administering subgrants, recruiting students for service-learning opportunities, and producing brochures or manuals about service-learning. Although LSAHE grantees were not *required* to integrate service into for-credit courses, this approach was encouraged, and over three-quarters of grantees and subgrantees were involved in developing service-learning courses.

APPROACH TO THE EVALUATION

The authorizing legislation for CNS requires evaluation of LSAHE impacts on service providers (i.e., student volunteers), communities, and institutions. CNS contracted with RAND to conduct the national evaluation of LSAHE. The evaluation included a combination of qualitative and quantitative methods.

The unit of analysis for this evaluation is *LSAHE-supported programs*. Because institutions typically combined their CNS funds with other sources of support for service-learning and seeded an array of activities throughout the campus, one cannot determine which students, or how many, participated in service as a result of the LSAHE grant (or matching funds). Thus, the activities, outputs, and impacts described in this report cannot be *wholly* attributed to LSAHE. Nonetheless, our observations over the past three years indicate that LSAHE was a critical catalyst on many campuses for the initiation, growth, and enhancement of service-learning programs and courses.

The evaluation was designed to address five questions:

What work did LSAHE programs perform? In the area of direct service, the evaluation determined the numbers of students providing direct service through programs and courses that received partial support from LSAHE, the hours of service they provided, the distribution of effort among different types of service, and the immediate program "outputs," such as the number of people or organizations served. In the area of capacity building, the evaluation determined the kinds of capacity building activities that programs conducted and the immediate results of these activities, such as the numbers of new courses developed or the hours of technical assistance provided. The primary data source for this aspect of the evaluation was an annual survey of LSAHE program directors, called the Annual Accomplishments Survey, that asked about program structure, resources, activities, and outputs. Response rates exceeded 70 percent in each of the three years it was administered.

What were the impacts of participation in LSAHE on service providers? LSAHE was intended to promote student development, including students' academic learning, sense of civic responsibility, and life skills. Through a review of the literature on service-learning, discussion with practitioners, and direct observation, RAND defined four domains of possible student impacts for LSAHE: (1) academic skills, including disciplinary knowledge and general skills in writing, analytical thinking, and quantitative reasoning; (2) professional skills and preparation, including clarifying career choices and gaining career-specific skills and experience; (3) life skills, especially teamwork, leadership, and an understanding of diversity and multiculturalism; and (4) civic skills and participation, including a commitment to volunteer service. The primary data collection activity for this component of the evaluation was a student survey conducted in the spring of 1997 comparing students in LSAHE-supported service-learning courses to those in similar courses that lacked a service component.

What was the impact of the work performed by LSAHE programs on service recipients? This component of the evaluation addressed the "service" impacts of LSAHE. RAND approached this question by asking the community organization staff who coordinated or oversaw volunteer programs to assess the college student volunteers. These staff regularly observe the work of volunteers and are in a strong position to assess their effectiveness. Additionally, their perceptions are critically important to the long-term success of LSAHE and other collegiate service-learning programs, because such programs depend on cooperation from community organizations. The assessment of students' effectiveness as service providers was based on a conceptual framework that considered the students' contributions to the *community organization* and to *service recipients.* To collect this information, RAND conducted two surveys of a random sample of community organization staff, called the Community Impact Survey. Respondents rated the student volunteers' effectiveness on a variety of dimensions and also assessed their overall strengths and weaknesses as service providers.

What were the institutional impacts of LSAHE? This aspect of the evaluation assessed the level and extent of institutional support for service-learning among colleges and universities with LSAHE grants, particularly *changes* in these institutional supports during the LSAHE funding period. RAND focused on four categories of institutional change: (1) the number and variety of service opportunities for students, (2) the integration of service into courses and curricula, (3) institutional ability to sustain service-learning programs after LSAHE ended, and (4) relationships with community organizations. In addition, this component of the evaluation addressed institutional factors that facilitate or hinder strong collegiate service-learning programs. Data sources for this component of the evaluation included the Annual Accomplishments Survey, which contained items about how colleges and universities supported service-learning; the Community Impact Survey, which contained items about relations between community organizations and higher education institutions; and site visits to LSAHE institutions, which focused intensively on institutional issues.

What was the return on the LSAHE investment? An important evaluation goal was to determine if the costs of LSAHE-supported programs are justified by the benefits the programs provide. RAND's approach to this component of the evaluation focused on the benefits that communities and service recipients derive from LSAHE-supported programs. The evaluation addressed the question of whether communities would benefit more if the funds used to support these service programs were used instead to pay staff directly to provide the same services. The Annual Accomplishments Survey was the primary source of data about program costs, supplemented by interviews with grantees and reviews of CNS records. The Accomplishments Survey also provided data about benefits by indicating the hours and types of student volunteer service provided to communities.

WHAT WORK WAS PERFORMED BY LSAHE PROGRAMS?

Virtually all programs responding to the Annual Accomplishments Surveys engaged in activities designed to build institutional capacity for service programs. In fact, staff spent more time on capacity building than on direct service activities.

The most common capacity building activity was course development. Between 1995 and 1997, almost 3,000 new service-learning courses were established. An average grantee responding to the Accomplishments Survey developed three new service-learning courses per year of funding. Respondents expected that their institutions would continue to offer these courses, at least in the subsequent year. These courses were primarily intended to build students' civic skills and increase students' disciplinary knowledge and skills.

Two-thirds of programs responding to the Accomplishments Surveys were also involved in technical assistance, generally to K–12 schools, community agencies, or other colleges or universities. Programs involved in technical assistance provided about 100 hours of assistance in Fiscal 1997.

Although a relatively small number of grantees (18 to 26 per year) were involved in awarding subgrants, this activity had a substantial effect on LSAHE by greatly increasing the number of institutions with LSAHE funding. Survey results indicate that between 225 and 328 subgrantees were funded through consortia each year, most receiving small grants of

$5,000 or $6,000. In this way, about one in eight higher education institutions participated in LSAHE between 1995 and 1997.

Beyond these capacity building activities, Accomplishments Survey results indicate that more than four out of every five respondents involved students in direct service to communities. Most programs worked in multiple service areas. About three-quarters of programs with a direct service component devoted some time to service in the area of education, and over half worked in health and human needs. Only about one-third of programs served in the area of public safety.

Programs responding to the Accomplishments Survey reported that, on average, 60 students participated in course-based service-learning and ten in co-curricular service-learning in 1997. These students participated for about 12 weeks, providing a total of 2,650 hours of service.

Through their direct service, LSAHE-supported programs assisted over 3,000 schools and close to 4,000 teachers in Fiscal 1997. They conducted over 4,000 home health visits, conducted about 600 tests of environmental quality, and worked with over 2,500 juvenile or adult offenders. There is some evidence that the numbers of accomplishments increased between 1995 and 1997, although the data do not produce clear patterns.

WHAT WERE LSAHE IMPACTS ON STUDENT SERVICE PROVIDERS?

To address this question, RAND surveyed two groups of students at each of 28 schools: (1) students who had recently completed an LSAHE-supported service-learning course, and (2) students at the same institution who had enrolled in similar courses that did not include a service component. Seven hundred twenty-five service-learning and 597 comparison students completed the survey, for a total sample of 1,300 students. The 41 percent response rate to this survey indicates a need for caution in interpreting and generalizing findings. The analysis compared these two groups to determine whether students in service-learning courses reported stronger effects of the course on their civic participation, life skills, academic skills, and professional skills.

Results reveal that students in service-learning courses, compared to those in similar courses without a service component, report larger gains in civic participation (especially intended future involvement in community service) and life skills (interpersonal skills and understanding of diversity). Service-learning and comparison group students did not differ in their perceptions of the impact of their course experience on academic and professional skills. Other results:

- There is little evidence that service-learning courses are less demanding than comparison courses. Results indicate that, relative to comparison courses, the service-learning courses required more writing and more time devoted to the course. In addition, there were no differences between the expected course grades for the service-learning students and the comparison students.
- Service-learning respondents were more satisfied than the comparison respondents with their courses. About two-thirds of the service-learning

respondents described their course as "above average" or "one of the best courses I've ever taken" compared to about 55 percent of the comparison group respondents.

- A majority of the service-learning respondents in all types of institutions participated in some kind of "reflection" on the service experience, including writing papers, keeping journals, and analyzing the causes of the social problems their service addressed. Respondents also reported that their courses involved periodic efforts to link the service experience to course content. Service-learning courses also included other kinds of learning opportunities, particularly exposure to diversity and teamwork.
- Students who reported relatively strong effects of service on their development were more likely than others to report that their course linked the service experience to course content. They were also more likely to volunteer in organizations other than health care facilities or schools. Those who self-selected into service received higher scores than a "typical" service-learning student in three of the four outcome areas.
- Students who did not participate in any service received higher scores than a "typical" service-learning student in two of four outcome areas studied (with no difference in the other two). However, this negative finding is reversed for students who volunteer more than 20 hours, discuss service experience in class, and enroll in courses that link course content to service.

These results are generally consistent with other research showing small positive effects of participation in service during college. A conservative conclusion is that participation in service-learning does not appear to slow or hinder student learning and development and carries some modest benefits, particularly in the area of civic and life skills. A less conservative conclusion is that service-learning may have stronger positive effects on certain students when specific elements are in place, especially strong links between course content and the service experience.

WHAT WERE LSAHE IMPACTS ON SERVICE RECIPIENTS IN THE COMMUNITY?

Results from two Community Impact Surveys and 30 site visits indicate that students participating in LSAHE-funded programs made valuable contributions to the organizations in which they served. Students served in nonprofit agencies, schools, government agencies, and health care facilities.

Community organizations responding to the survey perceived the student volunteers as highly effective in helping their organizations and meeting the needs of service recipients. These organizations reported that through the efforts of the volunteers, they were able to improve the quality, intensity, and variety of services provided and increase the number of service recipients. Organizations also rated student volunteers as highly effective in promoting positive outcomes for service recipients across the four areas of community need identified by CNS: education, health and human needs, the environment, and public safety. More specifically:

- Community organization staff responding to the Community Impact Survey assigned high marks to the student volunteers from LSAHE-supported institutions. Respondents assigned the highest ratings to students' enthusiasm, ability to work with staff and clients, and interpersonal skills.
- Results of the Community Impact Survey indicate that student volunteers from LSAHE-supported institutions were perceived as superior to other volunteers and about equal in effectiveness to paid staff.
- Community Impact Survey respondents reported that as a result of the student volunteers from LSAHE-supported institutions, their organizations were able to improve the quality of services, provide more services to each recipient, increase the variety of services offered, reach more service recipients, and improve staff morale. The LSAHE student volunteers had no impact on the number and workload of paid staff; they also supplemented rather than replaced other volunteer support.
- Fully 90 percent of respondents to the Community Impact Survey believed that the benefits of working with college student volunteers outweighed the costs. Almost all would like to work with student volunteers again if given the opportunity.
- The effectiveness of student volunteers is hindered to some extent by problems with transportation, which can reduce volunteers' reliability and availability. Other problems are the limited duration of time students serve (e.g., one quarter or semester) and "disconnects" between students' availability and service recipients' needs (e.g., if the college semester ends before the high school students being tutored take their final exams). Nonetheless, community organizations' most common suggestion for improvement was to expand service programs.

Analysis of site visit data indicates several factors that promote strong relations between LSAHE-supported institutions and community agencies. These include (a) the presence of a reliable contact person within both the higher education institution and the community organization, (b) clear and realistic expectations of volunteer and community organization responsibilities to one another, (c) moving students from the classroom into the community as quickly as possible, (d) ensuring that placements benefit the community organization and provide meaningful work for students, and (e) resolving transportation and scheduling issues that can reduce students' reliability and create frustration on all sides.

WHAT WERE LSAHE IMPACTS ON INSTITUTIONS?

In addition to promoting student development and serving communities, LSAHE also sought to expand service opportunities for students, integrate service into course work, foster mutually beneficial relationships with community organizations, and promote sustainable programs. Results indicate that the majority of institutions receiving LSAHE grants expanded their service opportunities, integrated service into courses and curricula, and enhanced community relations. Whether these institutions will sustain service-learning once LSAHE funding ends is unknown at his point. Major findings:

- Over three-quarters of LSAHE grantees responding to the Annual Accomplishments Surveys developed new service-learning courses. Grantees showed considerable progress in this endeavor, developing close to 3,000 new service-learning courses between 1995 and 1997. Among respondents to the 1997 Accomplishments Survey, 76 percent offered service-learning courses in three or more disciplines; of these, half had achieved this after 1994, indicating a temporal association with LSAHE. Nonetheless, fewer than half reported that service-learning was included in their institution's core curriculum, suggesting that service-learning is not fully integrated into the academic enterprise.
- In addition, grantees expanded co-curricular service opportunities. For example, about one-third of grantees responding to the 1997 Accomplishments Survey had added service activities to their new-student orientation within the past three years.
- Both LSAHE program directors responding to the Accomplishments Surveys and community organization staff responding to the Community Impact Surveys indicated that LSAHE had contributed to building strong relations between campus and community. For example, over three-quarters of LSAHE program directors involved community organization staff in planning service programs; of these, three-quarters had initiated this practice since 1994, indicating a temporal association with LSAHE.
- Results give mixed indications about the prospects for sustainability. LSAHE-supported programs are heavily dependent on temporary funds, and fewer than half have dedicated staff or permanent budgets. Nonetheless, program directors were optimistic about their ability to sustain their programs, and our analysis of return on investment suggests that programs increased their matching funds as their LSAHE grant awards decreased in size.
- The site visits point to four factors that are essential to the establishment of a strong service infrastructure: service centers, faculty involvement, leadership, and a service tradition.

WHAT WERE THE RETURNS ON THE LSAHE INVESTMENT TO THE COMMUNITY?

A key question in assessing the federal investment in LSAHE is whether service-learning programs produce significant value in comparison to the resources invested. Though the true return on the investment should be realized over time, this evaluation considers only the three years between Fiscal 1995 and Fiscal 1997. Nevertheless, data provided by the same set of 27 direct grantees over three years indicate that programs produced a total value of service for communities that is close to the level of program expenditures, although value remains below expenditures over the first three years. Programs tended to increase the value of service over the course of three years, suggesting that LSAHE will bring a long-term positive return to communities beyond the three years studied. Moreover, the data also show that between Fiscal 1996 and Fiscal 1997, there was a modest but significant replacement of LSAHE funds by local matching funds, which suggests that programs are moving toward sustainability, thereby continuing to contribute to the communities.

In summary, LSAHE made substantial achievements in its first three years of operation. Community organizations were strongly positive about the contributions of student volunteers. The returns to the community on the LSAHE investment are moving in a positive direction. Institutional support for service-learning has increased. Further, students who participate in service report some modest positive effects.

ACKNOWLEDGMENTS

Most important, we extend our thanks to the hundreds of Learn and Serve America, Higher Education program directors who completed questionnaires, identified their community partners, and responded to ad hoc requests for information and clarification. We especially appreciate the additional days that a smaller number of program directors spent preparing for and hosting our site visits. Thanks are due as well to the many community organization staff and students who took the time to complete our questionnaires.

A number of RAND staff made valuable contributions to the evaluation, including Jan Hanley, Rodger Madison, Sue Polich, David Klein, Julie Brown, Susan Weinblatt, Jo Levy and others in the Survey Research Group, Lisa Neufeld, Frances Wang, Derek Diaz, Sara Robyn, Judy Rohloff, Sharon Koga, and Janie Young. The authors gratefully acknowledge their help.

Within the Corporation for National and Community Service, Chuck Helfer provided his customary helpful review of this and other documents in the project. His support and commitment contributed substantially to the project's success.

Tora Bikson, Eric Dey, and Jim Hosek provided thoughtful and constructive reviews that greatly enhanced the analysis and report. We appreciate their contributions. Laura Zakaras and Jeri O'Donnell further improved the report through their contributions to writing and editing. Their thoughtful and careful work made our results more accessible to readers.

Despite the assistance of so many, we, the authors, take full responsibility for any errors that may remain.

1. INTRODUCTION

BACKGROUND AND CONTEXT

Service-learning, the combination of volunteer service and education, is a form of experiential education that has been used in schools and colleges for more than 30 years. Over the last decade, educators and policymakers have shown increasing enthusiasm about service-learning, and the numbers of service-learning programs have increased substantially (Rhoads, 1998). Within higher education, service-learning has earned the support of grass-roots student movements (e.g., the student-initiated Campus Outreach Opportunity League, or COOL), a national coalition of several hundred college and university presidents sponsored by the Education Commission of the States (Campus Compact), a number of prominent educational associations (e.g., the American Association of Higher Education, American Association of Community Colleges, National Society for Experiential Education), and leading educators (including Ernest Boyer, past president of the Carnegie Foundation for the Advancement of Teaching, who recommended in 1987 that all students participate in service as part of their undergraduate program).

The appeal of service-learning lies in its promise to address a number of important and vexing social problems. The first problem is perceived inadequacies in American education, both K–12 and higher education. Various tests and assessments indicate that American students lag behind their counterparts overseas and are not acquiring the skills and knowledge expected of them (Wingspread Group on Higher Education, 1993). One solution to this problem lies in active learning, or strategies to boost students' involvement and engagement in education as a means of increasing both their motivation and their mastery of educational concepts. Numerous testimonials from teachers and students suggest that service-learning is particularly effective as an active learning strategy. It also is well suited to incorporating other strategies that are associated with educational improvement, including collaborative learning and interdisciplinary education (Boyer Commission, 1998).

The second problem that service-learning promises to address is increasing concern about our youths' preparation to meet the responsibilities of living in a democratic society, including staying informed about social and political issues, voting and other forms of participation in governance, and a sense of personal responsibility to serve one's community and nation (Barber, 1992; Rhoads, 1998). The low rates of voting and disinterest in politics among young people are perhaps the clearest indicators of this problem. By engaging students in service to their communities, service-learning may increase their knowledge and understanding of and direct involvement in civic affairs. It also conveys to students that educators and community leaders place a high value on community service and expect all individuals to participate.

A third problem that service-learning addresses is the lack of funding for needed social and environmental services. The level of public funding for education, health care, public safety, and environment, for example, leaves many needs unmet, and this gap is expected to grow in the future (Council for Aid to Education, 1997). Volunteer service is one way to fill this gap. Thus, service-learning may contribute directly to fulfilling societal needs and, if effective in increasing students' civic responsibility, will have long-term benefits by increasing the total pool of volunteers.

In response to the promise of service-learning as a way to improve education, promote stronger civic life, and address social needs, the federal government has provided programs and incentives for schools to develop or expand such programs. In 1990, the Bush administration established the Commission for National and Community Service. Three years later, during the Clinton administration, the National and Community Service Trust Act (signed into law on September 21, 1993) established the Corporation for National and Community Service (CNS) to operate three initiatives: Learn and Service America, AmeriCorps, and the National Senior Service Corps. Learn and Serve America comprises two programs: Learn and Serve K–12 , for elementary and secondary students; and Learn and Serve Higher Education, for undergraduate and graduate students. This report focuses on Learn and Serve America, Higher Education (LSAHE).

One of the features that distinguishes LSAHE from other service programs for college students, such as AmeriCorps, is its emphasis on service-learning, or the dual goals of promoting the development of service providers (i.e., undergraduate and graduate students) and meeting the needs of service recipients. CNS works toward these goals by awarding funds to higher education institutions and community-based organizations through a national competition. Between Fiscal 1995 and Fiscal 1997, approximately $35 million was awarded in this manner.

The National and Community Service Trust Act requires CNS to evaluate its programs and report the results to Congress (section 12651d). The LSAHE evaluation is required to address the effects of LSAHE on service providers, service recipients, and higher education institutions. It is also required to assess the returns on the nation's investment in LSAHE.

Beyond this mandate, evaluation is important because, to date, the promise of service-learning remains largely untested and unverified. Although testimonials abound, there is little empirical information about the effects of participation in service-learning, especially at the postsecondary level.

Moreover, service-learning does not have unanimous acclaim. Skeptics question whether it is realistic to expect a relatively modest intervention to have such profound effects. Some believe that service-learning waters down the curriculum and that the time students spend volunteering would be better spent on more traditional academic pursuits. The implementation of service-learning also presents many problems, ranging from the demands such programs place on faculty members' time to the quality of learning activities. Relatively few faculty—particularly tenured or tenure-track faculty—participate. Until they do, service-learning will remain a marginal educational activity within higher education.

This evaluation assesses the degree to which LSAHE achieved its objectives and, in particular, its effects on college student volunteers, those receiving service, and higher education institutions. Our findings carry broader significance, by expanding the information available about service-learning generally and addressing the claims of both proponents and critics.

ORGANIZATION OF THIS REPORT

This report is divided into eight chapters. This chapter has described the goals and context of the national evaluation. Chapter 2 provides the conceptual framework for the research presented in the rest of the report.

Chapter 3 addresses the question, What work was performed by LSAHE programs? Findings are based on the Annual Accomplishments Survey administered to all LSAHE program directors.

Chapter 4 responds to the question, What were LSAHE impacts on students? This chapter presents findings from surveys of students who participated in LSAHE-supported programs.

Chapter 5 deals with the question, What were the effects of LSAHE on service recipients? Findings are based on the Community Impact Survey administered to community organizations that engaged students from LSAHE-supported institutions and on 30 site visits to LSAHE-supported institutions.

Chapter 6 addresses the question, What were the institutional impacts of LSAHE? Using information collected from the Annual Accomplishments and Community Impact Surveys and site visits, this chapter describes the types of support that colleges and universities with LSAHE grants provide for service-learning. It also discusses the factors that hinder or facilitate the development of service-learning within the higher education sector.

Chapter 7 analyzes whether LSAHE-funded programs produce significant value for communities compared to the resources they consume. This chapter responds to the question, What was the return on the LSAHE investment?

The concluding chapter summarizes the major findings of the evaluation and presents recommendations.

2. CONCEPTUAL FRAMEWORK AND APPROACH TO THE EVALUATION

WHAT IS SERVICE-LEARNING?

The term *service-learning* refers to activities that combine volunteer work with education. "Service-learning combines a strong social purpose with acknowledgment of the significance of personal and intellectual growth in participants" (Giles, Honnet, and Migliore, 1991, p. 7). Almost all service-learning programs are sponsored by schools, ranging from the elementary grades through postbaccalaureate professional programs.

The "service" component of service-learning is any unpaid activity that is intended to assist individuals, families, organizations, or communities in need. Service in this context may involve work that requires little or no training, such as serving meals in a homeless shelter, or it may involve highly skilled work, such as providing medical or legal services to indigent individuals. The service experience may be a one-time special event, such as a cleanup day in the community, or a long-term commitment, such as spending one morning each week in a social service agency.

The "learning" component of service-learning involves structured efforts to promote the development of the volunteer, such as acquiring new skills or knowledge or reaching a deeper understanding of social problems. Learning may occur as part of a class (course-based), or it may occur as a co-curricular activity.[1] The learning activities are referred to as "reflection," because the volunteers are encouraged to reflect on their experiences as service providers. Typical reflection activities involve journal keeping, discussion, reading, and writing term papers.

Given this broad definition, it is not surprising that service-learning programs take many forms. Some examples:

- Elementary school children clear a weedy patch of ground and plant a vegetable garden. The activity supports the school's math and science curriculum as the children measure, weigh, and chart their progress and observe the transformation of seeds to mature vegetables. They donate their harvest to the local homeless shelter, which prompts a class discussion about why people are homeless.
- The members of a high school Spanish club volunteer in a Head Start program that serves many Spanish-speaking children. Although the students receive no academic credit for their volunteer service, the faculty advisor devotes a portion of each club meeting to discussing the students' experiences at the Head Start

[1]Course-based service-learning refers to community service activities that are incorporated into an academic course or curriculum in which students enroll. Extracurricular, or co-curricular, service-learning refers to activities outside a course.

center, ranging from their feelings about the children's circumstances to the meaning of Spanish words or phrases they did not understand.

- College students enrolled in a course on child development are required to volunteer for at least 25 hours in an elementary school, keep a journal about their experiences, and write a term paper that draws on their interactions with the children to explain theories discussed in class.
- Ophthalmology graduate students provide eye examinations for homebound elderly as part of their clinical requirement.

Service-learning is distinguished from community service or pure volunteerism by its emphasis on the development or growth of the service provider and its "direct connection to the academic mission" of the sponsoring college or university (Rhoads, 1998, p. 279). It differs from field studies or other forms of experiential learning by its emphasis on addressing social problems. In practice, however, the boundary between service-learning and other forms of volunteerism or experiential learning is fuzzy at best.

Throughout this report, we use the term *service-learning* to refer to any activity that involves students in volunteer work for educational purposes. When service-learning occurs as part of the formal curriculum, we use the term *course-based service-learning.* The terms *volunteerism* and *community service* are used to refer to service that is not intended or designed to promote the service providers' learning and development.

OUTCOMES OF SERVICE-LEARNING

Service-learning is expected to meet community needs and improve students' learning, growth, and development. To date, however, little research has been conducted to determine the extent to which these expectations are met.

Most of the existing research has focused on student outcomes of service-learning. Two longitudinal studies of the effects of volunteerism during college on student development found a wide range of positive effects. For example, in their analysis of 3,450 students attending 42 institutions, Sax, Astin, and Astin (1996) found that students who volunteered in college showed more positive outcomes than nonvolunteers on three dozen outcome variables spanning the constructs of civic responsibility (e.g., commitment to serving the community, intent to participate in volunteer work in the future), academic development (e.g., aspirations for advanced degrees, contact with faculty), and life skills development (e.g., self-rated leadership, understanding of community problems, interpersonal skills).[2] In a similar study of over 12,000 students, Astin, Sax, and Avalos (in press) found that many of the positive outcomes of participation in volunteerism during college persist up to nine years after graduation. Although these studies control for a variety of differences between volunteers and nonvolunteers, the results indicate that the two groups were quite different at entry to college, and the possibility that the outcomes are attributable to pre-existing

[2]This work was conducted under subcontract to RAND.

group differences cannot be dismissed. Additionally, these studies do not differentiate service-learning from community service or volunteerism.

Similar results emerged from another national study, which focused on course-based service-learning for undergraduates as opposed to co-curricular service-learning or volunteerism during college. These results indicated small but significant positive effects of participation in service on a range of outcomes, especially students' values and attitudes related to citizenship and social justice and their self-rated skills (Eyler, Giles, and Braxton, 1997). Again, large differences between participants and nonparticipants prior to the service experience were observed.

Other studies focus on more limited samples. Many suffer from severe methodological deficiencies. Among the strongest is a study by Markus, Howard, and King (1993) in which students enrolling in a political science course at the University of Michigan were randomly assigned to service or nonservice conditions. Relative to the control group, those with the service experience showed greater gains in tolerance of others, desire to find socially useful careers, and application of course principles to new situations. They also had higher attendance rates and higher grades. While the use of experimental methods adds strength to this study, the small sample size (37 service-learning students) and, more important, the fact that the researchers taught the course suggest a need for caution. A number of other studies use post-test only designs to assess differences between students in service-learning programs and others (e.g., Cohen and Kinsey, 1994; Greene and Diehm, 1995). The weakness of this design coupled with small samples, weak instrumentation, and the high probability of selection biases renders such work of little value for summative evaluations.

Qualitative research on student outcomes has also been conducted. Rhoads (1998), for example, in a study based on participant observation and interviewing, describes the contribution of service-learning to students' understanding of themselves and others, including an enhanced appreciation of diversity and multiculturalism. He also found that participation deepened students' understanding of citizenship, societal problems, and the "social good." Ostrow (1995) discusses the effects of a service-learning experience on students' attitudes toward the homeless. He found that students showed increased empathy and greater understanding of the individual and societal factors that produce homelessness.

Even less research has addressed the effects of service-learning on communities and service recipients. Some practitioner-oriented materials emphasize the importance of college-community relations and provide tips for building partnerships (Kupiec, 1993; Tice, 1994), but such practical advice has not, to our knowledge, been empirically validated, nor has any research to date undertaken study of the community outcomes of collegiate service programs.

In sum, there is limited empirical support for the claims made about the benefits of service-learning. The existing research suggests that participation in service has small but significant and fairly widespread positive effects on students' levels of civic responsibility (variously defined, but generally including their interest in service to society), self-rated skills, and involvement in their education. This is consistent with other research about the benefits of experiential learning (Boyer Commission, 1998; Study Group on the Conditions of Excellence in American Higher Education, 1984).

THE LSAHE APPROACH

LSAHE emphasizes the links between service and academic learning by supporting the development of service-learning programs as part of undergraduate, graduate, and professional academic programs.

LSAHE Goals

Although the specific wording and structure of LSAHE goals differed in each fiscal year, three common themes emerge. In each year, LSAHE sought:

(1) To engage students in meeting the unmet needs of communities;
(2) To enhance students' academic learning, their sense of social responsibility, and their civic skills through service-learning;
(3) To increase institutional support and capacity for service-learning, as manifested in the number, quality, and sustainability of opportunities for students to serve.

Each of these is discussed below.

Engage students in meeting the unmet needs of communities. CNS identified four priority areas for service through LSAHE: (1) education, including service to facilitate school preparation and school success; (2) health and human needs, such as services to improve health and health care and more general "quality of life" services for low-income individuals, seniors, or people with disabilities; (3) public safety, including service to prevent crime or improve communities' response to crime (e.g., assisting crime victims); and (4) environment, including "natural" environments such as parks or stream beds and "neighborhood" environments such as housing complexes or downtown business districts. In practice, most but not all service fell into these categories.

Enhance students' academic learning, their sense of social responsibility, and their civic skills through service-learning. "Academic learning" refers to the acquisition of discipline-based knowledge and skills. For example, by tutoring high school students in algebra, college students might improve their own math skills. By volunteering in a homeless shelter, students might develop a better understanding of sociological, psychological, or political theory. Or by helping to restore an ecosystem, students might develop a better understanding of chemistry.

LSAHE also aims to strengthen students' "sense of social responsibility," or to increase their resolve to address societal needs through volunteer, professional, civic, or political service. A sense of social responsibility also refers to a felt obligation to fulfill one's responsibilities as a citizen and community member, although there is little consensus on what these responsibilities are beyond following the law and voting in elections.

Similarly, LSAHE strives to improve students' "civic skills," or the ability to serve effectively. Unfortunately, both CNS and the general literature on service-learning are quite vague about what civic skills entail, although teamwork, leadership, interpersonal skills, and an understanding of diversity issues as well as specific service skills (e.g., tutoring or mentoring) are typically included.

In practice, programs with LSAHE support embraced an even broader set of learning goals. Many programs included personal growth for students among their learning goals, such as helping students select majors or careers and promoting moral development or self-esteem. Additionally, like other experiential education programs, service-learning is often intended to increase students' commitment to and involvement in education through active learning.

Increase institutional support and capacity for service-learning. In addition to serving communities and improving students' learning, programs with LSAHE support were expected to promote institutional change and, in particular, to boost college and university support for service-learning, such as increasing the numbers of academic courses with service-learning components, the number of faculty teaching such courses (especially tenured or tenure-track faculty), and the level of institutional funding for service-learning activities. In so doing, LSAHE hoped to ensure that participating colleges and universities would sustain their service-learning programs after LSAHE grants terminated. In addition, by modeling "good practices" in service-learning, programs with LSAHE support were expected to boost the quality of *all* institutional service programs, such as transforming community service to service-learning programs, strengthening reflection activities, or improving community relations.

LSAHE Program Activities

Colleges and universities with LSAHE grants used these funds to support an array of service-learning courses and extracurricular programs. LSAHE funds were typically combined with other sources of support for service-learning and used to seed a number of service initiatives throughout the campus. For example:

- One college used its LSAHE grant to pay part of the salary for a staff person in a service-learning center. The center supported a wide variety of service-learning and community service programs, including individual internships, extracurricular activities, and service-learning courses.
- A larger LSAHE grant was used to infuse service throughout a college curriculum. In addition to adding a service component to a required course for freshmen, the grant indirectly helped build support for service-learning in higher-level courses, and once faculty agreement was secured, the program director used grant funds to help the academic departments develop service opportunities for upper division students.
- Another university used its LSAHE grant to cover the costs of releasing several faculty from part of their normal teaching load so they would have time to learn about service-learning and develop new courses with service components. The program staff provided workshops and individual assistance to help the faculty in

course development. Although the grant was over before the courses were offered, the program staff were prepared to continue assisting the faculty by placing and monitoring the student volunteers.

In each of these examples, the LSAHE grant increased the overall campus involvement in service-learning by enabling the institution to undertake new initiatives and extend or enhance existing activities.

Although LSAHE grantees were not *required* to provide service-learning through for-credit courses, this approach was encouraged, and over three-quarters of programs with LSAHE grants either developed new courses with a service component or modified existing courses to incorporate service. These courses spanned a wide variety of disciplines and postsecondary levels, from lower division courses for freshmen to advanced professional courses for graduate students.

Regardless of whether service-learning was provided through courses or co-curricular programs, LSAHE encompassed two broad types of activities: direct service and capacity building.

- *Direct service* activities were intended to engage students in meeting community needs and promote student learning. LSAHE-supported staff and faculty placed, trained, supervised, and monitored student volunteers, coordinated service programs, and taught service-learning courses. Reflection was an integral component of direct service, inseparable from training and supervision. The majority of participating LSAHE institutions provided direct service to a variety of community organizations, addressing two or more of the four key areas of service.
- *Capacity building* activities were intended to strengthen institutional support for service-learning and increase the number, variety, and quality of service opportunities for students. These activities included designing courses, establishing databases of service opportunities, providing workshops for faculty about service-learning, helping others develop service-learning programs, administering subgrants, recruiting students for service-learning opportunities, and producing brochures or manuals about service-learning.

About four out of five programs with LSAHE support provided or organized direct service activities. Staff in these programs devcted about one-third of their time to direct service activities. Virtually all programs engaged in some form of capacity building, and staff spent about half their time on these activities. The remaining staff time was devoted to administrative duties.

LSAHE Structure

Higher education institutions participated in LSAHE as direct grantees, subgrantees, or subsubgrantees. There are two types of direct grants:

(1) *Single institution* grants were awarded to one organization (almost always a college or university, but a handful of community agencies with specified college or university partners as well).

(2) *Consortium* grants were awarded to a group of institutions linked to a central hub that competitively subgranted part of the LSAHE award to other colleges and universities. Some of these subgrantees then awarded subsubgrants to still other colleges and universities. The consortium "hubs" rarely engaged in direct service and instead engaged in capacity building activities on behalf of their subgrantees. Some but not all consortia shared common themes (e.g., service to seniors or migrant workers, medical or legal services, integrating service-learning into undergraduate curricula).

As shown in Table 2.1, RAND identified between 365 and 458 total LSAHE direct grants, subgrants, and subsubgrants each year.[3] About three-quarters of LSAHE programs were funded through subgrants from consortia.

Table 2.1

Numbers of Various Types of Grants and Colleges Receiving LSAHE Funds Between Fiscal 1995 and Fiscal 1997

	Fiscal 1995	Fiscal 1996	Fiscal 1997
Single institutions	90	80	66
Consortium hubs	26	18	18
Consortium subgrants or subsubgrants	344	306	281
Total	460	404	365

In total, RAND identified 502 different organizations that participated in LSAHE between Fiscal 1995 and Fiscal 1997. Of these, 435 were higher education institutions or associations (the remainder were community-based organizations or independent consortium "hubs"). This means that about one in eight colleges and universities nationwide participated in LSAHE between Fiscal 1995 and Fiscal 1997.

The overall LSAHE program includes a relatively small number of institutions with relatively large grants, and a larger number of institutions with much smaller grants. On average, consortium hubs received the largest grant awards (most were over $100,000), while subgrantees and subsubgrantees received the smallest awards (about $5,000). The median size of direct grants was $72,464 in Fiscal 1995, $85,000 in 1996, and $68,776 in 1997.

Roughly half the LSAHE grantees, subgrantees, and subsubgrantees for which data were available were research universities or comprehensive universities, leaving liberal arts

[3]To identify subgrantees, we called all direct grantees and asked them to provide information about any subgrants they may have awarded; we then repeated this process to identify subsubgrantees. Because these kinds of self-reports are subject to some error, results are presented as approximations.

colleges and community colleges somewhat underrepresented within LSAHE relative to their distribution in the higher education sector overall.[4] Over half were public institutions. The geographic distribution of participating institutions corresponded closely to the geographic distribution of higher education institutions, with most grantees and subgrantees in the eastern and western regions of the country and a smaller number in the central and southern regions.

EVALUATION OF LSAHE

CNS identified five evaluation questions for LSAHE:

(1) What work was performed by LSAHE programs?
(2) What were the impacts of participation in LSAHE on service providers?
(3) What was the impact of the work performed by LSAHE programs on service recipients?
(4) What were the institutional impacts of LSAHE?
(5) What was the return on the LSAHE investment?

Question 1 focuses on the activities of programs with LSAHE support. Questions 2 through 5 address the effectiveness of service-learning as it was implemented through LSAHE.

RAND's evaluation of LSAHE was intended to answer these questions and thereby determine whether the program had achieved its national goals. However, because LSAHE placed few restrictions on the structure or design of its grantees' service-learning activities, the evaluation has significance for service-learning generally, not just LSAHE. By comparing different types of programs and institutions, the evaluation also indicates some of the factors that hinder or facilitate effective programs. The evaluation does not, however, indicate whether LSAHE is more effective than other approaches to service-learning, nor does it indicate whether service-learning is more effective than other pedagogical methods.

The unit of analysis for this evaluation is *LSAHE-supported programs*. Few LSAHE grants were used to support discrete service programs. Instead, institutions typically combined their CNS funds with other sources of support for service-learning and seeded an array of activities throughout the campus. For many—probably most—colleges receiving LSAHE support, it was not possible to determine which or how many students participated in service as a result of the LSAHE grant (or matching funds). Thus, the activities, outputs, and impacts described in this report cannot be *wholly* attributed to LSAHE. Nonetheless, our observations over the past three years indicate that LSAHE was a critical catalyst on many campuses for the initiation, growth, and enhancement of service-learning programs and courses.

---

[4]Thirty-two percent were comprehensive universities, 24 percent were liberal arts colleges, 21 percent were community colleges, and 18 percent were research universities.

Against this backdrop, the evaluation considers the effects of LSAHE-supported programs on individual students, communities, and institutions (questions 2, 3, and 4 respectively). RAND's approach to the evaluation is based on several common elements:

- First is the use of *multiple methods*, including quantitative and qualitative approaches to evaluation. RAND used more than one data collection method to address each of the evaluation questions. Surveys provided standardized, quantitative data that could be aggregated and compared in a structured manner. Interviews and observation through site visits provided a richer and more in-depth understanding of local programs. When different methods lead to similar findings, our confidence in the accuracy of the results increases (a process known as triangulation).
- The evaluation also reflects *multiple perspectives*. Rather than relying exclusively on program staff for information, we also collected data from community organizations, students, faculty, and higher education administrators.
- In addition to aggregating findings over all programs with LSAHE grants, the evaluation examined differences among programs as a function of geographic, institutional, and programmatic variables. Two factors—institution type and grant type—emerged as particularly important in explaining variation in the findings. These comparisons are discussed in more detail in the section on data analysis provided later in this chapter.

What Work Was Performed by Programs with LSAHE Support?

Approach to the Evaluation. This aspect of the evaluation describes (a) the activities undertaken by LSAHE-supported programs, and (b) the immediate outcomes of these activities. In the area of direct service, the evaluation determined:

- The numbers of students involved in direct service through LSAHE-supported programs and the hours of service they provided;
- The distribution of effort within and across programs among the four key areas of service (education, health and human needs, environment, and public safety);
- The immediate "outputs" of these service activities, including the numbers of people, families, or organizations receiving service.

In the area of capacity building, the evaluation determined:

- The kinds of capacity building activities in which programs were engaged;
- The immediate "outputs" of these service activities, such as the numbers of new courses developed or the hours of technical assistance provided.

Information about the work performed by LSAHE-supported programs was critical to our ability to interpret outcome data. For example, without this information we could not determine whether programs that failed to enhance student learning were unsuccessful because they failed to involve students in service or because the intervention itself did not have the intended effects. Similarly, this information helped us identify the factors that hinder or facilitate success.

Data Sources. To address this question, RAND conducted an annual survey of LSAHE program directors, called the Annual Accomplishments Survey. Additional information was obtained from a series of site visits in which researchers directly observed program activities and interviewed staff, faculty, students, and other participants.

What Were the Impacts of Participation in LSAHE on Service Providers?

Approach to the Evaluation. LSAHE was intended to promote student development, including students' academic learning, sense of civic responsibility, and life skills. As discussed above, operational definitions of these concepts are largely lacking. Through a review of the literature on service-learning, discussion with practitioners, and direct observation, RAND defined four domains of possible student impacts for LSAHE:

- *Academic Skills.* Participation in service-learning is expected to affect students' disciplinary skills and knowledge and general academic skills in writing, analytic thinking, and quantitative reasoning. By promoting involvement in learning and deepening students' understanding of course content, service-learning may also lead to increases in students' grades.
- *Professional Skills and Preparation.* Many service-learning programs seek to help students clarify or confirm their choice of major and career, as well as gain career-specific skills and experience. In so doing, the service-learning experience may boost students' confidence in themselves and commitment to completing their educational program.
- *Life Skills.* Service-learning experiences are also expected to help students develop their interpersonal skills, including both teamwork and leadership. Another important life skill these experiences are to promote is understanding diversity, e.g., people of a different background, race or ethnicity, national origin, or economic status from one's own.
- *Civic Skills and Participation.* An important goal of most LSAHE-supported service-learning programs was to teach students the importance of volunteer service and increase students' future involvement in service. Many practitioners hope that the service experience will have "spillover" effects on other forms of civic involvement, such as political activism or professional activities directed toward solving social problems.

Data Sources. The primary data collection activity for this component of the evaluation was a survey of students who enrolled in LSAHE-supported service-learning courses in Spring 1997. Additional information was obtained from interviews and focus groups conducted with students during site visits.

What Was the Impact of the Work Performed by LSAHE Programs on Service Recipients?

Approach to the Evaluation. This component of the evaluation addresses the "service" impacts of LSAHE-supported service-learning programs. Because students in LSAHE-supported programs served at literally thousands of different sites and engaged in hundreds of different service activities, it was impossible to directly assess the effects of their work on service recipients. Even if we had focused on a limited number of service-learning programs, findings could not be generalized to LSAHE overall.

We therefore chose to address this evaluation question by asking the community organization staff who coordinated or oversaw volunteer programs to assess the college student volunteers. This approach has several advantages for the LSAHE evaluation. These staff regularly observe the work of volunteers and are in a strong position to assess their effectiveness. They have no "stake" in the LSAHE evaluation results and hence are likely to be unbiased in their assessments. Additionally, their perceptions are critically important to the long-term success of LSAHE and other collegiate service-learning programs because such programs depend on cooperation from community organizations.

The assessment of students' effectiveness as service providers was based on a conceptual framework that considered the students' contributions to the *community organization* and to the *service recipients*. From this perspective, the major issues of interest included:

- The degree to which the volunteers enhanced the community organization by enabling it to reach more people, provide more service, improve quality of service, or improve the organizational climate (e.g., morale);
- The degree to which the volunteers contributed directly to achieving the goals of the community organization and meeting societal needs, such as helping children learn, improving public safety, or preventing illness;
- The differences between volunteers from institutions with LSAHE grants and other service providers, including other volunteers and paid staff;
- Community organization staff assessments of volunteers' strengths and weaknesses, and the staff's overall satisfaction with the volunteers and interest in continuing to work with the college or university.

Data Sources. To collect this information, RAND conducted two surveys of a random sample of community organization staff, called the Community Impact Survey. In addition, site visits included interviews with community organization staff and direct observation of students providing service.

What Were the Institutional Impacts of LSAHE?

Approach to the Evaluation. This aspect of the evaluation assessed the level and extent of institutional support for service-learning among colleges and universities with LSAHE grants, particularly *changes* in these institutional supports during the LSAHE funding period. Based on the LSAHE goals and early observations of LSAHE-supported programs, RAND focused on four categories of institutional change:

- The number and variety of service opportunities for students;
- The integration of service into courses and curricula;
- Institutional ability to sustain service-learning programs after LSAHE ended;
- Relationships with community organizations, including social service agencies, schools, and other service providers.

In addition, this component of the evaluation addressed the lessons learned from LSAHE regarding institutional factors that facilitate or hinder strong collegiate service-learning programs.

Data Sources. The Annual Accomplishments Survey of program directors included a series of items about how colleges and universities supported service-learning. A survey of community organization staff supplemented the Accomplishments Survey in the category of relations between higher education institutions and community organizations. A series of site visits to LSAHE institutions focused intensively on institutional issues.

What Was the Return on the LSAHE Investment?

Approach to the Evaluation. An important evaluation goal was to determine whether the costs of LSAHE-supported programs are justified by the benefits the programs provide. This component of the evaluation poses numerous conceptual and methodological problems. In particular, some benefits cannot be easily quantified, such as improving students' learning or sense of social responsibility. RAND's approach to this component of the evaluation focused on the benefits that communities and service recipients derive from LSAHE-supported programs. The evaluation addresses the question of whether communities would benefit more if the funds used to support these service programs were used instead to directly pay staff to provide the same services.

Consistent with our unit of analysis—programs with LSAHE support—we did not limit program costs to the LSAHE grant, but also included matching funds and other funds used to support these programs, including overhead. The benefits are based on the equivalent wage rates for the work performed by volunteers in LSAHE-supported programs, such as tutoring, counseling, providing legal or medical services, cleaning parks or trails, and so forth. The cost-benefit ratio indicates whether LSAHE-supported programs are cost effective from a community perspective in the short run. To obtain a longer-term perspective, it is necessary to determine whether communities continue deriving benefits from LSAHE-supported programs even after funding declines or ends. Thus, the evaluation also considers the likelihood of program sustainability.

Data Sources. RAND's annual survey of program directors (Accomplishments Survey) was the primary source of data about program costs, supplemented by interviews with grantees and reviews of CNS records. The Accomplishments Survey also provided data about benefits by indicating the hours and types of student volunteer service provided to communities.

METHODOLOGY

Table 2.2 shows the relationship between the five evaluation questions and the primary data sources, which are described in detail below. This section also outlines the data analysis used in the evaluation and discusses a few caveats to keep in mind when reading this report.

Table 2.2

Relationship Between Data Collection Activities and the LSAHE Evaluation Questions

Evaluation Questions	Accomplishments Survey[a]	Community Impact Survey[b]	Student Survey[c]	Site Visits[d]	Secondary Data[e]
What work was performed by LSAHE programs?	X			X	X
What was the impact on service recipients?		X		X	
What were the impacts on service providers?			X	X	
What was the impact on institutions?	X	X		X	X
What were returns on the LSAHE investment?	X	X			X

[a]Administered in Fiscal 1995 to 1997.

[b]Administered in Fiscal 1995 and 1996.

[c]A UCLA survey was administered in Fiscal 1995; a RAND survey in year 3.

[d]Ten site visits were conducted in each of Fiscal 1995 to 1997; Fiscal 1997 also included telephone follow-ups of 18 sites.

[e]Data sources include the National Center for Education Statistics and America's Job Bank (an on-line national job bank).

Annual Accomplishments Surveys

RAND surveyed all LSAHE program directors—direct grantees, subgrantees, and subsubgrantees—on an annual basis to address the question, What work was performed by LSAHE programs? The survey instrument collected four categories of information:

(1) Descriptive information about LSAHE grantees and programs, including program organization, resources, and staff members' use of time;

(2) Activities intended to build institutional capacity for service, including course development, technical assistance, and publications;

(3) Activities intended to serve the unmet needs of communities, including the numbers of student volunteers and service hours and their service activities;

(4) Service “outputs” (e.g., number of schools provided with tutors or recycling programs established) in four service areas.

The items initially were based on content analysis of LSAHE grantees’ proposals, program descriptions, and plans. As additional information was obtained about LSAHE activities, the items were revised, particularly the service “outputs.”

Response rates exceeded 70 percent each year. More specifically, in Fiscal 1995, 341 programs responded, for a 78 percent response rate; in Fiscal 1996, 327 programs responded, for a 77 percent response rate; and in Fiscal 1997, 262 programs responded, for a 72 percent response rate.

Community Impact Surveys

RAND conducted two surveys of a random sample of community organizations that served as host sites for student volunteers from LSAHE institutions. Survey questions asked respondents to assess the contributions of student volunteers from a designated “partner” college or university. The survey questions focused on (1) descriptive information about the community organizations involved in LSAHE, and (2) community organization assessments of the student volunteers from a designated partner LSAHE college or university, including the students’ (a) effects on the organization, (b) effects on service recipients, and (c) strengths and weaknesses as service providers.

Items assessing students’ effects on the service organization and strengths and weaknesses as service providers were based on reviews of the literature about effective service programs (e.g., Kupiec, 1993; Tice, 1994) and early site visits. Items assessing students’ effects on service recipients were designed to articulate with the service “outputs” included in the Accomplishments Survey.

RAND originally intended to survey community organizations each year of the LSAHE program. However, the Fiscal 1997 survey was dropped from the evaluation plan for several reasons. First, the results from Fiscal 1995 and Fiscal 1996 were very similar. Second, the ratings were so high that there was no opportunity for tracking further increases in respondent satisfaction. (Although it was possible that satisfaction could decline in the third year, the site visits strongly indicated that this was not the case.) Third, evaluation resources were shifted to enable RAND to address some emerging issues in greater detail than was provided for in the original evaluation plan.

In Fiscal 1995, 443 community organizations, or 69 percent of those surveyed, returned the questionnaire. In Fiscal 1996, 404 organizations responded, representing a 64 percent response rate.

Student Surveys

The evaluation included two student surveys, both intended to explore the impacts of LSAHE participation on student volunteers. The first survey, done in Summer 1995, was conducted by the UCLA Higher Education Research Institute as part of its ongoing series of longitudinal student surveys (The Cooperative Institutional Research Program). Over 3,000 students from 42 institutions with LSAHE grants completed this survey, for a 21 percent response rate. The second survey, conducted by RAND in Summer 1997, compared students enrolled in LSAHE-supported courses with those enrolled in nonservice courses. Over 1,300 students from 28 institutions with LSAHE grants completed this survey, for a 42 percent response rate.

Site Visits

To gain a more in-depth understanding of LSAHE-supported programs, the evaluation included ten site visits per year.[5] Site visits typically included two to three researchers, who remained on site for two to three days. During that time, researchers interviewed program staff, faculty, administrators, and community agency staff. They conducted student focus groups and observed students either in class or at their service sites. Follow-up telephone interviews were conducted with 18 sites one to two years after the site visits to determine how the programs had developed.

Data Analysis

The survey data were analyzed in two ways. First, results were aggregated across all respondents to provide an overview of LSAHE as a whole. Second, subgroups of respondents were compared (using chi square, multiple analysis of variance, multiple regression, or log linear regression, as appropriate) to determine how LSAHE-supported programs differed as a function of various factors.

Initial comparisons were based on nine factors that might influence evaluation findings:

- Geographic:
  - (1) Location of institutions with LSAHE-supported grants
    - east
    - south
    - central
    - west
  - (2) Urbanicity
    - urban
    - suburban
    - rural
- Institutional:
  - (1) Public versus private colleges and universities
  - (2) Institutional type
    - community colleges
    - liberal arts colleges

---

[5]Staff from the UCLA Higher Education Research Institute participated in 19 of the 30 site visits.

        - comprehensive universities
        - research universities
- Programmatic:
    - (1) Number of years institution had received LSAHE funding
        - first year
        - second year
        - third year
    - (2) Grant type
        - consortium hub
        - single institution direct grant
        - subgrantee and subsubgrantee
    - (3) Grant size (in dollars)
    - (4) Area of service provided
        - education
        - health and human needs
        - environment
        - public safety
    - (5) Fiscal year
        - 1995
        - 1996
        - 1997

Geographic and institutional data were obtained from reference materials, including a national database of information on higher education institutions maintained by the U.S. Department of Education. Programmatic data were obtained from CNS or RAND's surveys.

Four of these factors were dropped after the first year of data collection and analysis. Data on the number of years an institution had received LSAHE funding were unreliable because some institutions received different subgrants each year, others moved from direct grantees to subgrantees or vice versa, and so forth. Similarly, the area of service provided was dropped because the vast majority of programs provided service in two or more areas. Third, the variable for grant size was dropped because grant size data for subgrantees and subsubgrantees were unreliable and because grant type explains most of the variation in grant size. Finally, urbanicity was dropped because different data sources showed high levels of disagreement about the classification of higher education institutions as urban, suburban, or rural. Responses also indicated that many suburban and rural institutions were providing service in nearby urban areas while some urban institutions had service programs in rural areas, further confounding such classifications.

Analyses of the remaining five stratification variables were conducted for all datasets. Only two factors made substantial contributions to explaining variation in the results. First, a large number of differences emerge among consortia, single institution direct grantees, and subgrantees. This is consistent with observations that indicate these categories had quite different goals and resources. Second, many differences emerge as a function of institutional type, reflecting the large differences in organizational context and resources captured by these categories. Few differences by the other factors emerged, and in most cases this is no different than what one would expect by chance alone. In our presentation of evaluation results, therefore, only comparisons that achieved statistical significance are presented. In addition, we present findings by fiscal year, indicating the stability or change in results as a function of the year in which they were gathered. For the most part, the data show a high level of consistency across years.

Caveats

The methods used in this evaluation do not support causal conclusions about the impact of LSAHE on students, communities, or institutions. Rather, we can and do demonstrate the *associations* between LSAHE and certain kinds of outcomes, including changes in students' self-rated knowledge, skills, and attitudes; community organizations' capacity for and contributions to meeting societal needs; and institutional support for service-learning.

The evaluation also depends heavily, although not exclusively, on self-reports of respondents. For example, results regarding the number of students providing service, service hours, and service outputs are based on self-reports of LSAHE program directors or community organization staff, and no efforts have been made to verify their accuracy. Similarly, rather than measure students' knowledge via tests, the assessment of student outcomes is based on students' self-reports about how they believe their service-learning course affected them. Such perceptions may under- or overestimate the actual effects of LSAHE participation.

Additional caveats are provided as needed in the chapters that follow.

3. WHAT DID LSAHE PROGRAMS ACCOMPLISH?

INTRODUCTION

In order to understand the effects of LSAHE on students, communities, and institutions, it is necessary to understand the activities and accomplishments of programs receiving LSAHE support. By "accomplishments" we mean the short-term outputs that programs generated with LSAHE support. These include such outputs as courses modified or created to incorporate service-learning, numbers of students engaged in service activities, and numbers of children tutored. We do not attempt to measure accomplishments in terms of the effects of these program activities, such as increased test scores of children receiving tutoring or academic improvement by students engaged in service activities. Further research is needed to capture these types of accomplishments as well.

With this definition in mind, this chapter describes the major accomplishments of the LSAHE programs. The Annual Accomplishments Survey was the primary data source. RAND administered this survey each spring to program directors from all identified LSAHE direct grantees, subgrantees, and subsubgrantees. Response rates ranged from 78 percent in Fiscal 1995 to 72 percent in Fiscal 1997.

In addition to the caveats presented in Chapter 2, several issues specific to this chapter should be raised. First, respondents used diverse and often ad hoc criteria for defining LSAHE participants and programs and hence for attributing specific accomplishments to LSAHE. Second, due to possible overlap in accomplishments from one year to the next, it is inappropriate to aggregate the three years of data in an attempt to obtain an overview of LSAHE accomplishments across all three years.[1] Third, the Accomplishments Surveys do not provide a true longitudinal picture of LSAHE grantees between Fiscal 1995 and 1997, primarily because of considerable turnover among grantees at all levels. Rather, the survey was designed to provide a series of cross-sectional snapshots of LSAHE accomplishments. Taken together, the results demonstrate the types of achievements that higher education institutions with service-learning courses and programs can reasonably expect. We did, however, review results for 36 direct grantees that had returned relatively complete Accomplishments Surveys in each year. Trends emerging from this review are described below.

The results that follow are divided into three sections: (1) accomplishments related to building institutional capacity for service, including new service-learning courses, publications, and subgrants; (2) accomplishments related to direct service, such as hours of service provided and numbers of service recipients; and (3) the numbers of outputs in four

[1]For example, if a grantee reported serving 20 high schools each year, we cannot determine whether it served the same 20 each year or a different set of 20. Thus, the actual number of schools served over three years would be somewhere between 20 and 60.

service areas, such as numbers of health clinics assisted and numbers of water and soil samples taken for environmental testing.

PROGRAM ACCOMPLISHMENTS IN CAPACITY BUILDING

LSAHE-supported programs comprise a multiplicity of components, some of which involve direct volunteering by students and others that develop institutional capacity for community service. Across the three years of data collection, virtually all of the programs responding to the Accomplishments Survey engaged in some form of capacity building. Table 3.1 displays the proportion of responding programs undertaking different types of capacity building activities during the three years.

Table 3.1

Percentage of Respondents Including Various Capacity Building Components

Program Component	Fiscal 1995 (N=341)	Fiscal 1996 (N=313)	Fiscal 1997 (N=253)
Create service-learning courses	70	79	86
Provide technical assistance	69	54	66
Produce publications	50	56	62
Award and administer subgrants	12	15	14

Creating Service-Learning Courses

The percentage of programs involved in creating or modifying service-learning courses increased from 70 percent in Fiscal 1995 to 86 percent in Fiscal 1997. In total, 725 new courses were developed with LSAHE support in 1997, compared with 1,150 courses in 1996 and 1,035 courses in 1995.[2] By way of illustration, Table 3.2 provides the distribution of courses for Fiscal 1996.

Table 3.2

Percentage of Respondents Developing Various Numbers of New Courses in Fiscal 1996

Number of New Courses Developed	Percentage of Respondents
1 through 3	53
4 through 6	19
7 through 12	16
13 or more	11

[2]The survey employed a slightly different format each year to collect data on the number of new courses. Consequently, caution must be exercised when comparing these numbers from year to year.

On average, programs developed or modified three courses each year, spanning a wide range of disciplines. Not surprisingly, consortia were much less likely than other direct grantees, subgrantees, and subsubgrantees to develop service-learning courses.

A review of responses provided by 36 direct grantees who had responded to this question in the Accomplishments Survey in each year suggests that institutions made long-term investments in course development. Over two-thirds (70 percent) developed one or more new service-learning courses in each of the three years.

Programs also made strides toward sustaining their new service-learning courses. Among those programs that had developed new service-learning courses, the percentage that intended to offer some or all of the new courses the following year ranged from a low of 71 percent in Fiscal 1997 to a high of 91 percent in Fiscal 1995. Table 3.3 displays these results in more detail. The declining percentage of respondents who plan to continue all their new courses and the increasing percentage who are unsure probably reflect uncertainty about future funding.

Table 3.3

Percentage of Respondents That Plan to Continue All, Some, or None of Their New Service-Learning Courses

New Courses That Will Be Offered Again	Fiscal 1995 (N=341)	Fiscal 1996 (N=313)	Fiscal 1997 (N=253)
All	83	65	49
Some	8	19	22
None	2	3	5
Don't know	7	14	24

In most cases, LSAHE support enlarged rather than initiated course-based service-learning. Survey results for Fiscal 1996 indicate that a median of 60 students per campus enrolled in service-learning courses that received LSAHE support, while 163 students per campus enrolled in *any* service-learning course offered by the institution. A similar pattern emerges for Fiscal 1997: a median of 78 students per campus enrolled in service-learning courses that received LSAHE support, while 200 students per campus enrolled in *any* service-learning course offered by the institution. In other words, 39 percent of service-learning enrollments on an average campus were at least partially supported by LSAHE.

Despite a common focus on course-based service-learning across LSAHE, grantees approached this task with widely differing goals and expectations. The 1996 Accomplishments Survey asked respondents to indicate the primary educational goals of their service-learning courses. Table 3.4 displays results. These results indicate that while program directors commonly engaged in the activity of creating new courses, their goals and expectations for these courses varied widely.

Table 3.4

Service-Learning Course Goals Endorsed by 1996 Accomplishments Survey Respondents

Goals of Service-Learning Courses	Percentage of Programs Ranking Goal 1st, 2nd, or 3rd in Importance
Develop civic skills	49
Increase disciplinary knowledge and skills	46
Commit to community involvement	45
Build career-related skills and knowledge	33
Learn value of volunteer work	26
Learn how to create social change	24
Increase involvement in studies	22
Develop leadership skills	18
Enhance ethical and moral development	18

NOTE: Due to missing data, N=246.

Providing Training and Technical Assistance

Sixty-six percent of all programs responding to the Accomplishments Survey in Fiscal 1997, compared with 54 percent in 1996 and 69 percent in 1995, provided training or technical assistance to other organizations.[3] As we found in previous years, consortia were more likely to provide technical assistance than were other types of grantees. In 1997, for example, 93 percent of the responding consortia and 80 percent of other direct grantees provided training and technical assistance, compared to 60 percent of subgrantees and subsubgrantees. An average program provided 100 hours of technical assistance (median) in each of Fiscal 1996 and 1997, compared with 72 hours in Fiscal 1995.

Programs providing technical assistance were most likely to serve community-based organizations, K–12 schools, and colleges and universities within a consortium to which they belonged. The most popular topics for technical assistance were linking higher education institutions and community organizations, designing courses or integrating service-learning into curricula, supervising students involved in community service, and designing community service programs.

Producing Publications

An increasing percentage of respondents reported producing publications with LSAHE support over the course of three years. In Fiscal 1995, half the respondents produced publications with LSAHE support; in Fiscal 1996, 56 percent; and in Fiscal 1997, 62 percent. Most of the increase occurred among subgrantees and subsubgrantees. Forty-four percent of subgrantees and subsubgrantees produced publications with LSAHE support in Fiscal 1996, compared with 54 percent in Fiscal 1997. The types of publications produced included

[3]The survey defined technical assistance as "assistance, instruction, or consultation to educators, community representatives, or program managers and staff about community service or service-learning."

program brochures, newsletters, training information for volunteers, guides for developing service-learning programs and courses, and research and evaluation reports.

Awarding and Administering Subgrants

LSAHE direct grants were awarded to between 18 and 26 consortia in each year. Sample preparation for the Accomplishments Surveys identified between 225 and 328 subgrantees that were funded through these direct grantee consortia. As shown in Table 3.5, some subgrantees also functioned as consortia, awarding subsubgrants.

Table 3.5

Subgranting Activities

	Number of Programs[a]		
Grantee Type	Fiscal 1995	Fiscal 1996	Fiscal 1997
Consortia that were direct grantees	26	18	18
Subgrants awarded by direct grantee consortia	272	254	225
Consortia that were subgrantees	16	13	19
Subsubgrants awarded by subgrantee consortia	72	52	56

[a]Adding the number of subgrants and the number of subsubgrants awarded (the second and fourth rows of this table) equals the number of consortia subgrants reported each year (see the third row of Table 2.1).

Accomplishments Survey results indicate that each consortium awarded a median of 14 subgrants in Fiscal 1995, declining to six subgrants in Fiscal 1997. The total dollars each consortium awarded averaged $51,000 in Fiscal 1995, $21,230 in Fiscal 1996, and $19,237 in Fiscal 1997 (median). The median size of an individual subgrant or subsubgrant was $6,000 in Fiscal 1997, compared to $5,000 in prior years.

Those programs involved in subgranting faced a number of special responsibilities. Since subgrants were awarded competitively, these programs needed to solicit and review proposals. They disseminated funds to their subgrantees (or subsubgrantees) and collected fiscal and programmatic reports from them. They also provided technical assistance, and most convened annual conferences to bring all their subgrantees or subsubgrantees together.

PROGRAM ACCOMPLISHMENTS IN DIRECT SERVICE

In addition to capacity building activities, most LSAHE-supported programs engaged in direct service, or activities that directly involve students in providing service to communities. The percentage of Accomplishments Survey respondents that included direct service in their grant-related activities ranged from a low of 78 percent in Fiscal 1995 to a high of 88 percent in Fiscal 1997.[4] The outputs of those providing direct service can be

[4]Breaking down the 12 percent of respondents that did not include direct service in their Fiscal 1997 program by grantee type, we find nine consortia, one single institution direct grantee, and 19 subgrantees or subsubgrantees.

measured in several ways: numbers of service providers, service hours, and service recipients; and community needs that specific service activities addressed. Each of these is addressed below.

Numbers of Service Providers, Hours, and Recipients

Students perform service activities either as part of an academic course or as a co-curricular activity. The 1996 and 1997 Accomplishments Surveys asked respondents to report the numbers of students whose participation in service-learning courses or programs was at least partially supported by LSAHE funds.[5] As shown in Table 3.6, in 1996, programs reported engaging a median of 40 students for 12 weeks in course-based service-learning, totaling 1,300 hours for the year. In 1997, programs reported a larger median number of students (60) and, not surprisingly, a higher median number of hours (1,650). In co-curricular service, programs engaged fewer students on average (four in 1996 and ten in 1997), though they reported a proportionately larger median number of hours of service (1,000 in both 1996 and 1997).

Table 3.6

Measures of Student Involvement in LSAHE-Supported Programs and Courses

	Fiscal 1996	Fiscal 1997
Course-based Service		
Median number of students per program	40	60
Median number of weeks students participated	12	12
Median hours of service per program	1,300	1,650
Co-curricular Service		
Median number of students per program	4	10
Median number of weeks students participated	12	11
Median hours of service per program	1,000	1,000

Through their volunteer efforts, responding LSAHE-supported programs served a median of 300 people per program in each of Fiscal 1996 and Fiscal 1997. Caution must be exercised in reporting and using these numbers, however. Data reported by 20 percent of respondents in 1996 and 28 percent in 1997 were discarded because respondents indicated that they counted service recipients more than once (e.g., if they received more than one session or type of service). Consequently, these results are based on a small sample size with a considerable amount of missing data.

Community Needs Addressed

Table 3.7 shows the distribution of Accomplishments Survey respondents' service activities across the four priority areas of community need defined by CNS: education,

[5]Fiscal 1995 data are not reported here, because no distinction was made between co-curricular and course-based service and because the wording of the items about service participants created considerable ambiguity.

health and human needs, neighborhood and natural environment, and public safety. In each year, at least two-thirds of respondents worked in multiple service areas and only 12 percent reported working outside these four areas.

Table 3.7

Percentage of Accomplishments Survey Respondents Providing Direct Service in Various Service Areas

Area of Community Need	Fiscal 1995	Fiscal 1996	Fiscal 1997
Education	77	75	71
Health and human needs	60	63	55
Neighborhood and natural environment	46	50	47
Public safety	37	35	32
Other	12	12	12

Base = Respondents providing direct service.
NOTE: Percentages sum to over 100 percent because most grantees worked in multiple areas.

As shown in Table 3.7, the majority of programs involved students in service in education as well as in meeting health and human needs. Over half of the programs provided service in the neighborhood and natural environment area, while a third of responding programs provided direct service in public safety activities.

SPECIFIC ACCOMPLISHMENTS

This section describes LSAHE grantees' reported accomplishments in four areas of community need.

Education: School Readiness, School Success, Parenting, and Literacy

The goals of educational work were to further early childhood development, improve the educational achievement of school-age youth, and promote adult literacy. Programs working in the area of education in Fiscal 1997 reported that students devoted the most time to teaching classes or providing in-class support (18 percent) and to acting as mentors or role models for youth (18 percent). Students also spent a significant portion of their time providing out-of-class tutoring (15 percent). Those were the three most popular activities for last year's respondents as well. Table 3.8 displays some of the education outputs reported by programs that responded to the Accomplishments Surveys.

Health and Human Needs

In the area of health and human needs, the goals were to provide comprehensive community health care and prevention services and to help homeless, impoverished, elderly or disabled individuals. Programs working in this area in Fiscal 1997 devoted the most time to providing health education; offering companionship or chore support for elderly, ill, or disabled individuals; and providing meals or other services to homeless families or individuals. Table 3.9 displays a sample of the health-related outputs reported by respondents.

Table 3.8

Accomplishments in the Area of Education

Individuals or Organizations Receiving Service	Number Served		
	Fiscal 1995	Fiscal 1996	Fiscal 1997
Preschools	226	340	220
Elementary schools	928	1,099	1,800
Middle or junior high schools	358	763	605
High schools	254	540	538
Teachers	1,877	3,700	3,925

Base = Respondents providing service in the area of education.
NOTE: The total numbers served are less than the sum of the three years because many organizations and individuals received services in multiple years.

Table 3.9

Accomplishments in the Area of Health and Human Needs

Type of Service	Number Served		
	Fiscal 1995	Fiscal 1996	Fiscal 1997
Home visits	735	8,254	4,027
Assisting in health facilities (e.g., clinics or hospitals)	218	629	793
Homeless individuals placed in residence	67	256	101

Base = Respondents providing service in the area of health and human needs.
NOTE: The total numbers served are less than the sum of the three years because many organizations and individuals received services in multiple years.

Programs involved in the area of health and human needs were more likely to be found at community colleges than at other types of institutions. Relatively few consortia addressed health and human needs.

Neighborhood and Natural Environment

The goals of service efforts in neighborhood and natural environments were to promote improvements in neighborhoods and conserve, restore, and sustain natural habitats. In keeping with the previous two years, the programs that organized direct service activities to promote environmental improvements devoted the most time in Fiscal 1997 to cleanups, tree plantings, and other park and neighborhood revitalization efforts. After revitalizing efforts, students spent their time educating others about the natural environment and sampling, performing tests, mapping, and monitoring natural resources. Table 3.10 displays the environmental accomplishments reported by programs that responded to the Accomplishments Surveys.

Table 3.10

Accomplishments in the Area of Environment

Type of Service	Number Served		
	Fiscal 1995	Fiscal 1996	Fiscal 1997
Samples or tests of air, water, and soil conducted	75	2,915	596
Parks, gardens, or outdoor recreation areas established or improved	124	253	287
Public lands improved	215	103	107
New homes built	27	115	61
People educated about the environment	4,839	21,408	14,382

Base = Respondents providing service in the area of environment.
NOTE: The total numbers served are less than the sum of the three years because many organizations and individuals received services in multiple years.

Public Safety: Crime Prevention and Response, Legal Assistance, and Conflict Resolution

The goals of service in the area of public safety were to reduce violence in schools and communities, improve law enforcement and victim services, and offer legal services, mediation, and conflict resolution. Programs that sought to enhance public safety through crime prevention and crime response in Fiscal 1997 devoted the most time to teaching conflict resolution or helping mediate disputes. In addition, they provided gang diversion services, such as after-school programs and substance abuse prevention education. These were the most popular activities in the prior year as well. Table 3.11 displays some of the outputs in the area of public safety reported by responding programs.

Table 3.11

Accomplishments in the Area of Public Safety

Type of Service	Number Served		
	Fiscal 1995	Fiscal 1996	Fiscal 1997
Dispute resolution assistance for children	Not available	4,706	3,224
Dispute resolution assistance for adults	Not available	697	350
Offenders or delinquents served	Not available	2,725	2,587
Crime victims served	Not available	533	1,047
Police departments receiving assistance	54	44	61
Victim assistance facilities served	72	284	75

Base = Respondents providing service in the area of public safety.
NOTE: The total numbers served are less than the sum of the three years because many organizations and individuals received services in multiple years.

While these numbers are impressive, we found that a small number of grantees accounted for a large proportion of service outputs. For example, in the area of health and human needs, three programs accounted for almost half of the low income or impoverished service recipients in Fiscal 1997, and another three programs accounted for 45 percent of the 13,788 senior citizens served in the same year.

As discussed earlier in this chapter, it is inappropriate to sum accomplishments across all three years. For example, we have no way to determine whether the 75 victim assistance facilities served in Fiscal 1997 were included among the 284 such facilities served the previous year.

Finally, we note that due to turnover in the samples from year to year, the results do not offer a longitudinal portrait of LSAHE. We did, however, review responses from 30 single institution direct grantees that had completed this section of the Accomplishments Survey in each year. Over one-third (36 percent) showed clear evidence of increasing service "outputs" in at least one major category. For example, a grantee that concentrated in the service area of health and human needs reported an increase in the number of student volunteers' home visits from 12 in Fiscal 1995 to 50 in Fiscal 1996 and 500 in Fiscal 1997. A grantee that concentrated on education reported an increase in the number of teachers served from four in Fiscal 1995 to 28 in Fiscal 1996 to 75 in Fiscal 1997. The remaining 64 percent of respondents either showed stable outputs or their service activities changed so much that we were unable to compare their results across the three years.

SUMMARY OF CONCLUSIONS

Subgranting Enabled More Institutions to Receive LSAHE Support

Each year between 18 and 26 of the direct grantees competitively awarded subgrants to other colleges and universities. RAND identified several hundred subgrantees each year, some of whom awarded additional grants to 44 to 56 subsubgrantees. Thus, the initial set of between 84 and 114 CNS awards each year eventually encompassed 435 higher education institutions, or roughly 12 percent of the nation's colleges and universities. Moreover, these institutions spanned a wide range of regions and institution types (public versus private universities, research universities versus liberal arts and community colleges).

LSAHE Program Staff Spent Most of Their Time on Capacity Building Activities

In terms of the resources programs devoted to various activities, capacity building activities maintained their importance over the three years of the evaluation. In implementing LSAHE programs, staff spent more time on capacity building activities than on direct services. They devoted between 33 and 37 percent of their time to training, supervising, or coordinating student volunteers, compared to about 50 percent of their time on building institutional capacity for service, primarily adding service-learning to courses and curricula, developing partnerships or networks regarding community service, and providing training and technical assistance regarding service-learning. Though one might have expected capacity building activities to taper off as programs matured, this division of staff time between direct service and capacity building remained constant over the course of the three years.

Integrating Service-Learning into Curricula Was the Single Most Common Capacity Building Activity

The percentage of responding programs integrating service-learning into courses and curricula increased steadily from 70 percent in Fiscal 1995 to 86 percent in Fiscal 1997. This increase reflects the program priorities CNS communicated to the grantees. Nearly 3,000 new service-learning courses were established using LSAHE support between Fiscal 1995 and Fiscal 1997. However, it is noteworthy that a decreasing number of respondents were confident that the courses they developed one year would still be offered the following year. This decline is most likely attributable to increasing uncertainty about funding.

Over Half the Respondents Also Provided Technical Assistance

Programs reported providing a median of 100 hours of technical assistance in Fiscal 1996 and 1997, compared with 72 hours in Fiscal 1995. Consortia were significantly more likely to provide technical assistance, while the single institution grantees tended to receive technical assistance. Subgrantees were the least likely both to provide and to receive technical assistance; subsubgrantees appeared to be completely out of the loop of technical assistance. This information should help target future technical assistance activities. However, it also raises questions about whether subgrantees are not interested in providing or receiving technical assistance or are hampered from doing so by obstacles such as finances and communication.

Most Programs Engaged in Direct Service to Communities and Individuals

Between 78 and 88 percent of respondents each year included some direct service in their LSAHE program. In Fiscal 1996 and 1997, these programs engaged on average between four and ten students per co-curricular direct service program and between 40 and 60 students per course-based direct service, serving an average of 1,000 total volunteer hours in co-curricular service and between 1,300 and 1,650 in course-based service. However, inconsistencies across and within programs in determining numbers of participants and numbers of service recipients call for caution.

Education Was the Most Common Form of Service

Seventy-five to 80 percent of the responding programs involving students in direct service worked in education. In particular, programs reported that students taught classes, provided in-class support, or acted as role models or mentors.

During the three years of data collection, many of the reported activities and numbers were consistent. Significant fluctuations in the data were most likely due to vagaries of reporting rather than to programmatic changes. This consistency validates our early findings and gives us confidence in highlighting these major findings.

4. WHAT WERE THE IMPACTS OF SERVICE-LEARNING ON STUDENTS?

INTRODUCTION

An important component of the LSAHE evaluation was the assessment of the LSAHE impacts on student development, including educational attainment, life skills, and civic responsibility. Because, as discussed earlier, there are few uniquely identifiable Learn and Serve students at the postsecondary level, this evaluation set out to address how participation in an LSAHE-supported program affected students.

Several different elements of the evaluation addressed this question. First, the Higher Education Research Institute (HERI) at UCLA conducted a special study for the LSAHE evaluation in 1996. This survey of 2,172 undergraduate students in 42 institutions found statistically significant, albeit modest, effects of service on a wide range of outcome measures spanning the areas of educational attainment, life skills, and civic responsibility. Students participating in service within LSAHE-funded institutions reported higher net gains than nonparticipants in such measures of civic responsibility as commitment to helping others, promoting racial understanding, and influencing social values and political structures. Student service providers also exhibited higher levels of academic achievement aspiration (e.g., pursuing doctoral or other advanced degrees) and involvement (e.g., studying, talking with faculty) than did nonparticipants. Student volunteers at LSAHE institutions also displayed higher scores than did nonparticipants on 13 different measures of life skills, including perceptions of leadership abilities and opportunities, social self confidence, interpersonal skills, and acceptance of other races and cultures. Although these results are generally consistent with those of other research about community service, a low response rate (21 percent) limits the degree to which findings can be generalized.[1] In addition, this study focused on the effects of participation in any form of volunteerism in LSAHE-supported colleges and universities, regardless of whether LSAHE actually supported the service activity and regardless of the link between the service activity and the institution's academic programs. Another limitation of this study is that the sample consisted of undergraduates in baccalaureate programs only and did not include graduate or professional students or students in community colleges.

Second, RAND conducted a survey of college students in the late spring and summer of 1997. This survey involved two groups of students at each of 28 schools: students who had recently completed a LSAHE-supported service-learning course, and students who had recently completed a similar course that did not include a service component. Across the 28 schools, 725 service-learning students and 597 comparison group students completed the questionnaires. The Student Survey asked students to report on a specified service-learning

---

[1]Results of this study are available on request from the Higher Education Research Institute or CNS.

or comparison course, including their experiences in and assessment of the course and their beliefs about how the course affected them. This chapter presents results of the Student Survey.

The next section of this chapter summarizes the RAND Student Survey methods. It is followed by a review of results organized around two broad areas of analysis:

- First, we describe the differences between respondents in the service-learning courses and respondents in the comparison courses, focusing on (a) student characteristics, (b) students' assessments of and satisfaction with their course, and (c) perceived effects of the course on students' (i) academic skills, (ii) professional skills, (iii) civic skills, and (iv) life skills.
- Then we look more closely at the respondents in the service-learning courses. We describe the reasons they enrolled, their course experiences, and their service activities. We also consider the factors that differentiate service-learning experiences with relatively strong perceived effects on students from those with weaker effects on students.

The chapter concludes with a summary and discussion of findings.[2]

SUMMARY OF METHODS

To address the question of LSAHE impacts on students, RAND administered surveys to students in LSAHE-supported service-learning courses and to a comparison group of students in similar courses that did not involve service. This section reviews the Student Survey methodology.

Service-learning courses were defined as courses in which students were required to serve or given the option of volunteering in community settings as part of their course-related work. In most cases, service-learning courses were paired with a comparison course offered by the same institution during the same academic quarter or semester. Comparison courses did not have a volunteer component but were similar to service-learning courses in other ways, including academic discipline and subject matter, level (lower division, upper division, or graduate), course enrollment, and units of credit.

RAND developed two survey instruments. One instrument was administered to students in service-learning courses, and the other was given to students in comparison courses. Each questionnaire asked respondents to focus on a specified course. The questionnaires included the following common questions: (1) background and demographic information about respondents, (2) respondents' history of involvement in community service, (3) respondents' assessments of the course, and (4) perceived effects of the course on

---

[2]Another source of information about student outcomes of LSAHE was a set of site visits to institutions with LSAHE grants, which included focus groups and individual interviews with student participants. Almost without exception, these students were very positive about their service experience, but since the students were handpicked by program staff to participate in the interviews, conclusions about program effectiveness cannot be drawn from them. The student interviews were very useful, however, in suggesting ways in which the service experience may influence students.

respondents' educational, professional, life, and civic skills. In addition, the questionnaire for students in service-learning courses contained items about their service experience.

The sample included students from six community colleges, three liberal arts colleges, nine comprehensive universities, and ten research universities. All 28 institutions were single institution direct grantees of LSAHE. In each school, between one and five pairs of comparable courses were identified, for a total of 144 courses. These courses spanned a wide range of disciplines, with psychology and English being most common.

The number of students enrolled in these courses was 3,376. The total number of Student Surveys returned to RAND was 1,378, for a 41 percent response rate. Fifty-six surveys were dropped from the analysis, yielding a total of 1,322 usable surveys. The response rate was slightly higher for the comparison group than for service-learning respondents (42 percent versus 38 percent). Table 4.1 displays the number of responses and distribution of respondents by institutional type.

Table 4.1

Distribution of Respondents by Institution Category

Institution Category	Number of Schools	Number of Service-Learning Respondents	Number of Comparison Respondents	Total Respondents
Research universities	10	283	199	482
Comprehensive universities	9	217	208	425
Liberal arts colleges	3	30	22	52
Community colleges	6	195	168	363
Total	28	725	597	1,322

Analysis of the Student Survey responses was conducted at three levels:

- First, we compared all service-learning respondents against all comparison group respondents.
- Second, we conducted these comparisons separately for each type of institution, enabling us to compare research universities, comprehensive universities and liberal arts schools,[3] and community colleges. (We present group differences only when they extend across most or all of the schools in each group, not when they are driven by a single institution within a group.)
- Third, we conducted a focused study of six schools (two schools from each of the three institutional types). The schools selected for this purpose had both a large number of respondents and a high overall response rate. These six schools

[3]Comprehensive and liberal arts schools were originally intended to be two separate categories, but because of the low number of responses from liberal arts colleges (52), the two types of schools were grouped together. The liberal arts respondents were 81 percent female, 98 percent under 30 years old (with 75 percent 21 or younger), and 90 percent white. These demographics are different from those of the rest of the comprehensive school population, as the next section will show, but the liberal arts respondents were nonetheless grouped with comprehensive respondents out of necessity.

(hereafter referred to as the "six select schools") provided 51 percent of all respondents (674 out of 1,322), with an overall response rate of 70 percent.[4]

We used two approaches to quantify differences between survey populations. The first approach utilizes the paired course structure of the data. Here we apply the nonparametric Wilcoxon sign-rank test to the difference between a statistic, such as the mean class response to a survey question, for each pair of service-learning and comparison classes. The second approach uses linear models to account for demographic and institutional differences before testing whether group membership (service-learning or comparison) is significant in predicting a response outcome.

Caveats

Due to the low response rate (and the probability of self-selection), results should be classified as a *quantitative case study* with conclusions limited to the Student Survey respondents. Although a low response rate does not always bias the results, caution is called for in generalizing findings beyond the sample to any larger population or individual school, program, or course. Indeed, because of the large nonresponse rate, we cannot even claim that these results well represent the complete course populations from which our Student Survey sample was drawn.

Another important caveat is that the Student Survey measures the *perceived* and not the *actual* impacts of the courses on students' development. Thus, respondents may under- or overestimate the true effects of participation in service-learning.

In spite of the low response rates, we found results that are fairly consistent across various levels of data aggregation. In particular, most of the aggregate results correspond well to the results from the six select schools, which as a group had a reasonably high response rate. This provides some reason to believe that the high nonresponse rate did not bias our aggregate results. We did, however, find evidence that many students self-select into service-learning courses, which introduces other biases.

DIFFERENCES BETWEEN SERVICE-LEARNING AND COMPARISON GROUP RESPONDENTS

This section describes differences between service-learning and comparison group respondents with regard to student characteristics, course assessments, and perceived impact of the course.

Differences in Respondent Characteristics

Demographics. The service-learning and comparison groups were similar on most demographic factors. The major difference is that the service-learning group had a higher proportion of females than did the comparison group (78 percent versus 68 percent). This

[4]The six schools are not listed separately, because one of the conditions for distributing the student survey was that schools would not be individually identified in reports of our results.

difference was most pronounced in comprehensive universities and liberal arts colleges and least pronounced in research universities. Table 4.2 displays these results. Other differences emerge when the data are broken down by institutional type. Within community colleges, service-learning respondents were more likely than comparison group respondents to attend school full-time and less likely to be working. Within four-year institutions, service-learning respondents were slightly older on average than comparison group respondents. (The service-learning group within comprehensive universities and liberal arts colleges included a lower proportion of African-Americans than did the comparison group. However, this difference is entirely attributable to the distribution of students from one historically black college, so no interpretation about the overall institutional type should be drawn.[5])

Table 4.2

Percentage of Respondents with Various Characteristics, by Institution Type

	Research University		Comp. and Liberal Arts		Community College		Aggregate Sample		Six Select Schools	
Characteristic	s-l (N= 283)	com (N= 199)	s-l (N= 247)	com (N= 230)	s-l (N= 195)	com (N= 168)	s-l (N= 725)	com (N= 597)	s-l (N= 307)	com (N= 367)
Sex										
Female	75	69	79	67	77	67	78	68	73	63
Age										
0-21	60	66	50	63	55	55	55	62	62	66
22-29	34	31	36	29	20	21	31	28	30	26
30+	7	4	13	8	25	23	13	11	8	8
Race										
White	71	73	75	56	43	46	65	59	42	45
African-American	4	4	16	35	11	4	10	16	16	23
Hispanic	15	13	6	4	32	30	16	15	26	19
Asian	6	6	2	1	3	7	4	4	7	6
Other	4	4	2	4	1	12	5	6	9	7
Degree										
AA/AS	2	3	2	2	72	69	20	21	27	20
BA/BS	85	95	75	89	23	23	65	72	65	77
Grad.	12	2	22	12	3	3	13	6	8	2
Other	0	0	1	0	3	4	1	1	1	1
Student Status										
Full-time	95	99	97	97	78	71	90	91	89	92
Employment										
Full/part-time	61	61	61	64	68	76	65	63	63	63

[5]Within the community colleges, *one school* accounts for 75 percent of African-American respondents and 61 percent of Hispanic respondents. Similarly, only one of the comprehensive and liberal arts schools accounts for 90 percent of the African-American respondents in this school category. And, within the research universities, one school accounts for 54 and 58 percent of the Asian and Hispanic respondents, respectively, and over 90 percent of African-American responses come from five schools. Thus, any analysis based on race is inextricably confounded with school effects.

Service History. The Student Survey asked respondents to describe their volunteer experiences during high school, college, and while out of school. As shown in Table 4.3, a surprising finding is that service-learning respondents were slightly *less* likely than the comparison respondents to have participated in community service during high school.[6]

Grades. Service-learning respondents reported slightly higher grade point averages (GPAs) than did comparison group respondents (an average of 3.16 for service-learning students versus 3.06 for the comparison students). This difference was not in evidence among respondents from research universities, but it did apply to respondents from other institutional types.

Table 4.3

Percentage of Respondents Who Were Never/Rarely or Occasionally/Often Involved in Community Service at Different Times, by Institution Type

Time of Involvement in Service	Research University		Comprehensive and Liberal Arts		Community College		Aggregate Sample		Six Select Schools	
	s-l	com	s-l	com	s-l	com	s-l	com	s-l	com
In high school										
Never or rarely	27	24	34	28	53	48	36	32	37	31
Occasionally or often	73	76	67	72	47	52	64	68	64	69
In college										
Never or rarely	25	25	24	43	30	55	26	43	27	47
Occasionally or often	75	75	76	57	70	45	74	57	74	53
While out of school										
Never or rarely	56	41	48	44	57	56	54	46	54	49
Occasionally or often	44	59	52	57	43	44	46	54	46	51

Distinguishing Characteristics of Service-Learning Courses

Respondents were asked to compare their service-learning or comparison course to other courses they had taken during the same academic year on such dimensions as the course difficulty and amount of work, level of contact with instructors and classmates, and overall value of the course. Comparisons between the service-learning and comparison groups using a Wilcoxon sign-rank test indicate only two factors that distinguish service-learning from comparison group courses at the aggregate level: (a) service-learning courses

[6]This differs from results of UCLA's 1996 survey, which showed a strong association between volunteer work during high school and volunteer work during college. A possible explanation for this difference is that the current study focused on students who volunteered as part of a course, while the UCLA study included both course-based and co-curricular service. Another possible explanation lies in differences in the samples, since the UCLA study excluded community college and graduate students. Because problems with both samples preclude generalizations, more research is needed to determine the importance of prior involvement in community service as a predictor of participation in postsecondary service-learning courses.

demanded more time from students than did comparison courses, and (b) service-learning courses involved more writing than did comparison courses (see Table 4.4).

Table 4.4

Mean Ratings of How Service-Learning Courses Compare to Other Courses Respondents Have Taken in the Same Year: Aggregate Sample

Course Characteristics	Service-Learning	Comparison Group
Time devoted to the course	3.6	3.4
Amount of writing	3.2	3.0

NOTES: Differences are statistically significant, $p < .05$. Ratings were provided on five-point scales, with 1 = "service-learning course has much less of the attribute than other courses," and 5 = "service-learning course has much more of the attribute than other courses."

A more complex portrait emerges when data are disaggregated by institutional type:

- Within research universities, service-learning courses involved more reading and writing than did comparison courses but less library work. Service-learning respondents in research universities also had less difficulty understanding service-learning course content.
- Within comprehensive universities and liberal arts colleges, service-learning courses relative to comparison courses involved more time and more writing, but less library work and less reading. Service-learning respondents in comprehensive universities and liberal arts colleges also reported higher rates of contact with their professors than did comparison respondents.
- Within community colleges, service-learning courses involved more time than did comparison courses, as well as more library work and less reading.

Thus, perceptions differed considerably as a function of the type of institution respondents were attending.

Student Satisfaction with Service-Learning Courses

Relative to the comparison group, service-learning respondents reported higher levels of satisfaction with their courses (see Figure 4.1). Breakdowns by institution type reveal that over 72 percent of service-learning respondents in comprehensive universities and liberal arts colleges rated the service-learning course as above average, compared to 47 percent of the comparison group. Within research universities, 60 percent of the service-learning respondents, compared to 51 percent of the comparison group respondents, assigned these high ratings. These differences do not appear at the community college level, however, with 77 percent of service-learning respondents and 76 percent of the comparison group rating their course above average.

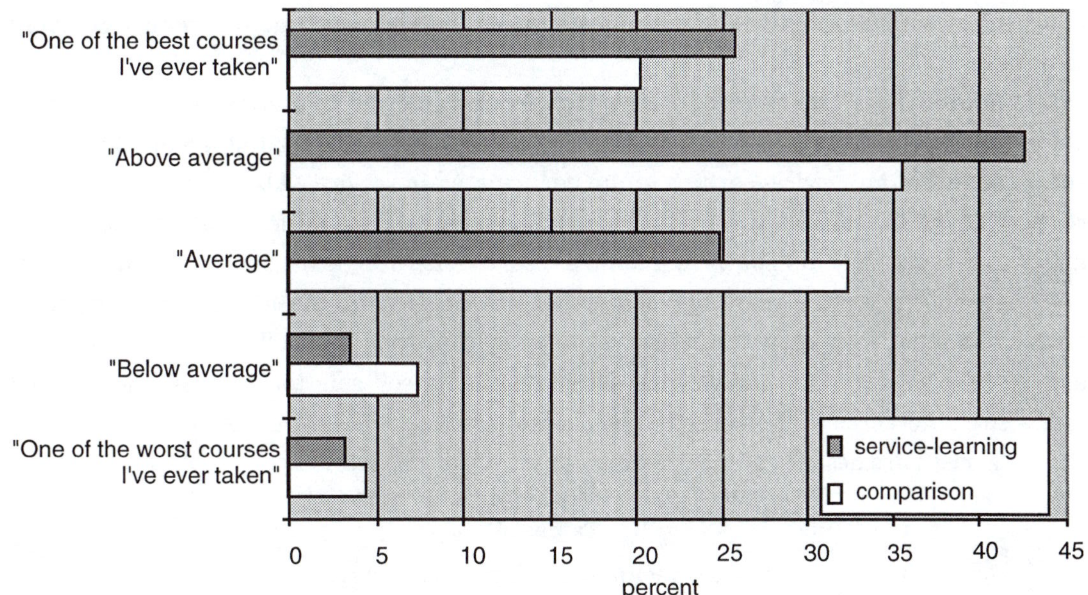

Figure 4.1—"Overall, how would you characterize the course?"

It is possible that respondents report higher levels of satisfaction with service-learning courses because the courses bring "an easy A" or place few demands on students. To test this hypothesis, respondents were asked to indicate the grade they received in the course (or to estimate, if their final grade was not yet known). Across all institutional types, there was no difference in expected or received course grades between the two respondent groups. Thus, there is no evidence that satisfaction is the result of especially lenient grading patterns in service-learning courses. In addition, the previous section suggests that service-learning courses are not perceived as significantly less demanding than other courses.

Influence of Service-Learning Courses

This section examines the impact of participation in course-based community service on students' self-reported skills and intentions. We describe how students believed the course influenced them, and we indicate whether those in service-learning courses perceived different effects than did those in comparison group courses.

In particular, this section describes the perceived effects of service-learning on four different dimensions: academic skills, life skills, professional goals and skills ("professional skills"), and continuing involvement and interest in community service ("civic participation"). These outcome measures were calculated as the average of sets of survey questions related to each dimension. Table 4.5 lists the items that constitute each outcome measure. The table also displays Cronbach's Alpha statistics, which show a high degree of intercorrelation among items within each area and therefore support the approach taken here to organizing the data.[7]

A Note About the Service-Learning Group. In order to understand the results that follow, it is important to highlight two aspects of the service-learning group. First, not every student in the service-learning group participated in service. About one-fifth of this group opted out of service altogether. The nonparticipants are not included in these analyses, because they did not have a complete service-learning experience. Second, about one-quarter of the service-learning respondents *self-selected* into the service-learning group, which means that they knew the course involved service prior to enrolling in it and wanted to participate in service. Our analyses compared results for self-selectors versus others, and we discuss the differences that emerged. The characteristics of those who opted out of or self-selected service are described in more detail later in this chapter.

Table 4.5

Outcomes Included in Regression Analyses

Academic Skills (Cronbach's Alpha = .78)
- Writing skills
- Analytic skills
- Disciplinary knowledge
- Quantitative skills

Professional Skills (Cronbach's Alpha = .64)
- Confidence in your choice of major
- Confidence in your choice of career
- Preparation for your career
- Expectation that you will complete your educational program and graduate
- Confidence in your own skills and abilities

Life Skills (Cronbach's Alpha = .86)
- Interpersonal skills
- Understanding people of a different background from your own

Civic Participation (Cronbach's Alpha = .84)
- Your current level of involvement in activities addressing social problems
- Expectation that you will become involved in addressing social problems in the future
- Your current level of involvement in campus activities or politics
- Expectation that you will become involved in campus activities or politics in the future
- Your current level of participation in national, state, or local politics
- Expectation that you will participate in national, state, or local politics in the future
- Expectation that you will participate in community service after completing your schooling

[7]Cronbach's Alpha is a measure of the correlations among items within a scale. Correlations among the four scales themselves ranged from .38 to .52, suggesting that the scales are measuring separate albeit related constructs.

Linear Model Results. We used multiple linear regression to compare service-learning and comparison group respondents in each of the four outcome areas, after controlling for sex, age, race, student status (full- or part-time), employment status, degree being sought, and institution type. The concept was to model an outcome variable based first on demographic variables in an attempt to account for as much of the variability as possible. Then, in the presence of these variables, we introduced a variable for service-learning or comparison group membership and tested whether this variable was statistically significant in predicting the outcome. In other words, we assessed the effects of participation in service-learning after controlling for other factors that may help to explain differences between the two groups.

The most interesting result is that the differences between the service-learning and comparison groups in the outcome areas of academic skills and professional skills are statistically insignificant, while the differences between the two groups in the outcome areas of life skills and civic participation are statistically significant *regardless of which other covariates are included or excluded from the models.* For example, even if none of the demographics are controlled for (an approach that greatly increases the likelihood of finding statistically significant effects of service-learning), the service-learning/comparison course covariate is insignificant for academic skills and professional skills. Conversely, even when all demographics are included in the model (an approach that reduces the likelihood of finding statistically significant effects of service-learning), the service-learning/comparison course covariate is still significant in the life skills and civic participation areas.[8] These results were consistent within each type of institution, as well as for the sample as a whole and the six select schools.

The results vary slightly when the service-learning respondents are divided into those who self-selected into the course and those who did not. Here we fit separate models for self-selectors versus the comparison group and for non-self-selectors versus the comparison group. The results described above are replicated when we compare the nonservice selectors against the comparison group (and this is true for both the aggregate sample and for the six select schools). In contrast, when we compare service selectors to the comparison group, we find that service-learning status is still insignificant in predicting the academic skills outcome, but is now significant for professional skills along with life skills and civic participation. However, this result occurs only for the aggregate sample, not for the six select schools. Thus, there seems to be a weak indication that service may be related to career aspirations for those who were seeking a service experience.

We note that the R^2 values for these models are all very small, ranging from 0.03 to 0.07. This implies that many factors other than those included in the analyses presented here affect students' responses to the Student Survey items about course outcomes.

---

[8]We did not apply more sophisticated hierarchical modeling techniques or adjust the standard errors for clustering, because (1) the results were strong and consistent across all levels of aggregation, and (2) the data do not support sophisticated model building. That is, because of problems such as the large nonresponse rate, we felt that it was only appropriate to look for trends and indications in the data.

Nonparametric Test Results. We also evaluated the same outcome variables at the aggregate level using the Wilcoxon sign-rank test. This tests for differences at the paired class level and accounts for demographic, class, and school differences in a different manner from the previous linear models. Yet here we find that the patterns continue to hold, with no difference between service-learning and comparison classes for academic skills and professional skills, and statistically significant results for life skills and civic participation. Table 4.6 shows results for all levels of data aggregation.

Table 4.6

Wilcoxon Sign-Rank p Values for the Difference Between Service-Learning and Comparison Courses, at Various Levels of Aggregation

	Outcome Variables			
Level of Aggregation	Academic Skills	Life Skills	Professional Skills	Civic Participation
All classes together	0.126	0.042[a]	0.846	0.002[a]
Community colleges	0.749	0.658	0.763	0.156
Comprehensive and liberal arts schools	0.368	0.125	0.750	0.033[a]
Research universities	0.148	0.278	0.206	0.278
Six select schools	0.468	0.029[a]	0.441	0.023[a]

[a]NOTE: $p < .05$.

The table shows that life skills and civic participation were both statistically significant for the aggregate sample ("all classes together") and for the six select schools. Civic participation was also statistically significant for comprehensive universities and liberal arts schools. Otherwise, the Wilcoxon sign-rank test did not have sufficient power to detect significant differences at the institutional level, although the pattern of p values suggests that a detectable difference may exist given more data.

Since past research has demonstrated strong effects of participation in community service on civic responsibility, we applied the Wilcoxon sign-rank test to each of the component questions in the civic participation outcome area. Table 4.7 shows the results. At the aggregate level, results indicate that political activity is least associated with service-learning, while campus activity and involvement in societal problem solving are moderately associated. The expectation of participation in future volunteer work or community service shows the strongest association with service-learning.[9] This pattern holds at the institutional level and for the six select schools. In spite of the loss of power with disaggregation, all categories except community colleges show statistically significant differences for the expectation of future participation in community service.

---

[9]These results represent self-reported impressions and intentions at the time of the survey, not actual behavioral change, of course.

Table 4.7

Wilcoxon Sign-Rank p Values for the Difference Between the Service-Learning and Comparison Courses for Items That Make Up the Civic Outcome Variable, at Various Levels of Aggregation

	Research Universities	Comp. and Liberal Arts	Community Colleges	Aggregate Sample	Six Select Schools
Current involvement in addressing social problems	.049[a]	.015[a]	.237	.001[a]	.007[a]
Expected involvement in addressing social problems	.169	.294	.237	.018[a]	.003[a]
Current involvement in campus	.880	.026[a]	.056	.006[a]	.033[a]
Expected involvement in campus	.743	.096	.186	.035[a]	.167
Current involvement in politics	.397	.398	.992	.271	.238
Expected involvement in politics	.355	.750	.974	.747	.963
Expected involvement in service	.002[a]	.002[a]	.462	.0001[a]	.004[a]

[a]$p < .05$.

STUDENT EXPERIENCES IN SERVICE-LEARNING COURSES

This section focuses exclusively on the service-learning respondents, examining their reasons for enrolling in the course, course experiences, and the factors that help to explain differences among service-learning respondents in the four outcome areas of academic skills, professional skills, life skills, and civic participation.

Self-Selection into Service-Learning Courses

Fewer than one-third (30 percent) of the service-learning respondents were aware that their course involved community service before they signed up for it.[10] Of these respondents, 82 percent indicated that they "wanted to participate in service," with the remainder "neutral or undecided" about the service component.

Thus, these Student Survey results indicate that 24 percent of the service-learning respondents knew that the course involved service before it began and wanted to participate. In other words, they self-selected into the course. Self-selection is of methodological importance because it provides an alternative explanation to the effects of the course itself for observed differences between the service-learning and comparison groups. Self-selection is also relevant to policy issues, such as whether students should be required to enroll in service-learning courses. The results reported in the previous section, for example, suggest

[10]Out of 725 respondents, 106 did not answer this question. The majority of these (99) did not volunteer for or perform service as part of their class.

that self-selectors are more likely than other students to perceive service-learning as having a strong influence on their professional development.

Relative to other respondents in the service-learning group, self-selectors were more likely to be female (82 percent of self-selectors versus 77 percent of others), white (75 percent of self-selectors versus 62 percent of others), and to have volunteered "occasionally" or "often" during high school (71 percent of self-selectors versus 63 percent of others). These findings were observed both in the aggregate and for each of the institutional types.

Reasons for Enrolling

The questionnaire asked respondents to indicate why they enrolled in the service-learning course. As shown in Table 4.8, respondents were most likely to enroll because they were interested in the course and least likely to enroll because they thought the course would be easy. Although these self-reports are subject to social desirability biases, they are consistent with findings presented earlier suggesting that service-learning courses carry about the same workload as comparison group courses.

Table 4.8

Service-Learning Respondents' Reasons for Selecting the Course

Reason for Enrolling	Percent Enrolling for This Reason
I thought it would be interesting	59
I was interested in the subject matter	54
It was required	46
The instructor is a good teacher	34
It fulfilled a general education or breadth requirement	25
It fit my schedule	17
My friends were taking the course	6
I thought it would be easy	5

NOTE: Percentages sum to over 100 because respondents marked more than one reason.

Figure 4.2 compares the reasons self-selectors cited for enrolling in the course to the reasons the other service-learning respondents cited. The figure shows that the self-selectors were more likely to enroll because of interest in the subject matter, which they knew would encompass service and service-learning. In comparison, the nonselectors were more likely to have chosen the course because it fulfilled an academic requirement or for the convenience of their course schedule.

Extent and Nature of Respondents' Participation in Service

Of the 725 service-learning respondents, 65 percent reported that volunteer work was required as part of the course. Thirty percent of the respondents stated that volunteer work was a course option, and 5 percent stated that there was neither a requirement nor an

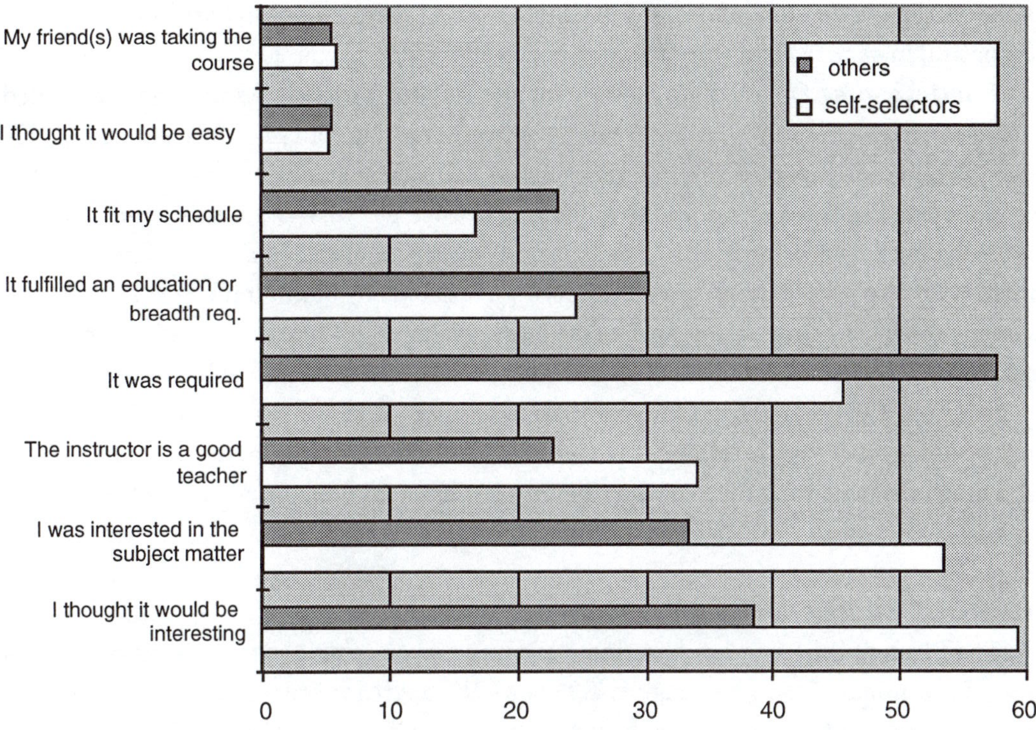

NOTE: Bars sum to over 100 percent because respondents checked multiple reasons.

Figure 4.2—"Why did you enroll in this survey course? (Check all that apply)"

option.[11] About 68 percent of the service-learning respondents indicated that they "wanted to participate in service" when asked what their attitude about the course service requirement was prior to beginning the course; 28 percent were neutral or undecided, and only 5 percent did not want to participate.

Nonparticipants. Twenty-one percent of the respondents in the service-learning courses indicated that they did not perform any volunteer service as part of the course. These students were asked why they did not participate. Sixty-six percent of the nonparticipants indicated that they did not have the time, 23 percent stated that they were already involved in community service, and 16 percent preferred a different option offered by the instructor.

Relative to those respondents who participated in community service as part of their course, the nonparticipant group had a higher percentage of males and was older. The age difference did not carry through to differences in respondents' current degree status (undergraduate versus graduate degrees), indicating that differences were based on age and not graduate student status. These results were confirmed by modeling the probability a service-learning respondent would not participate in the service aspect of the course using

[11]It is unclear what the 4.6 percent reporting that there was neither a requirement nor an option indicates. It is likely to be a mixture of respondents who did not understand the question, who did not understand course requirements, and who were in courses for which service-learning did not apply to some portion of the class.

logistic regression. In sum, males and students over 21 were more likely to opt out of participating in service than were females and students 21 or younger.

Participants. On average, those respondents who participated in service provided 20 hours (median) of community service over the duration of the course. Sixty percent of the service participants reported volunteering for less than three hours per week, and another 21 percent reported between three and five hours of service per week. Slightly over half volunteered for between ten and 16 weeks, representing an entire quarter or semester. Approximately 14 percent reported volunteering for between six and nine weeks, and about 35 percent reported volunteering for five or fewer weeks. Fifty-one percent of the student participants volunteered in a school, 32 percent volunteered for a public health organization (such as a hospital, health clinic, or senior citizen center), and the remaining 17 percent volunteered for other organizations, such as a legal clinic or environmental agency. These results are consistent with those of the Community Impact and Annual Accomplishments Surveys.

Placement, Training, and Supervision

The Student Survey queried service-learning respondents about their preparation and training for community service. Figure 4.3 shows the aggregate responses to the question, How did you select your volunteer or community service site? Practices varied widely by school. Within a few schools, almost all respondents reported being assigned to community organizations, while other schools seemed to leave the entire process of identifying and selecting the community organization up to the students.

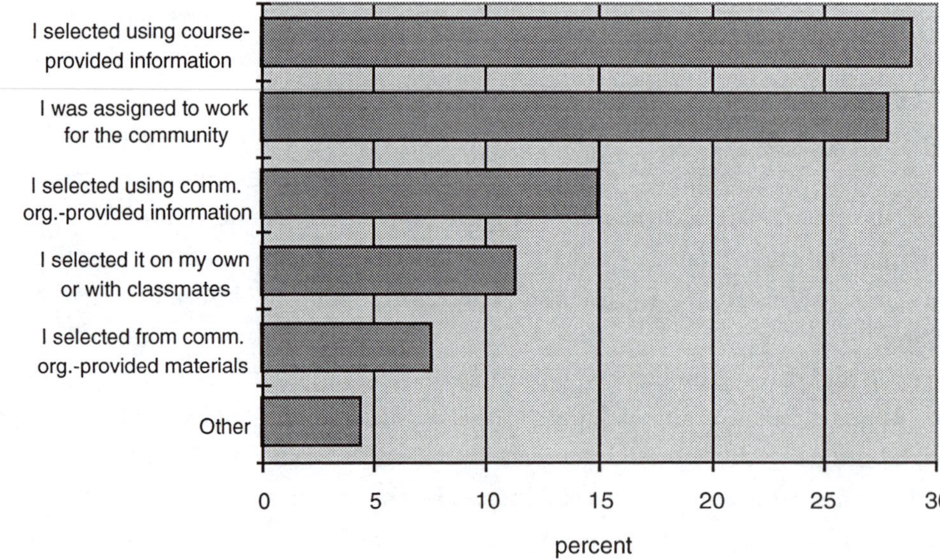

NOTE: Respondents could select more than one response.

Figure 4.3—"How did you select your volunteer or community service site?"

Figure 4.4 shows the type of training respondents received in preparation for their community service. Just over 20 percent of the respondents did not receive any training or orientation. Community college respondents were more likely to receive training from the community organization (47 percent), while respondents in comprehensive universities and liberal arts colleges were more likely to receive theirs from the course instructor (44 percent). Respondents in research universities were less likely to receive training from the course instructor (19 percent).

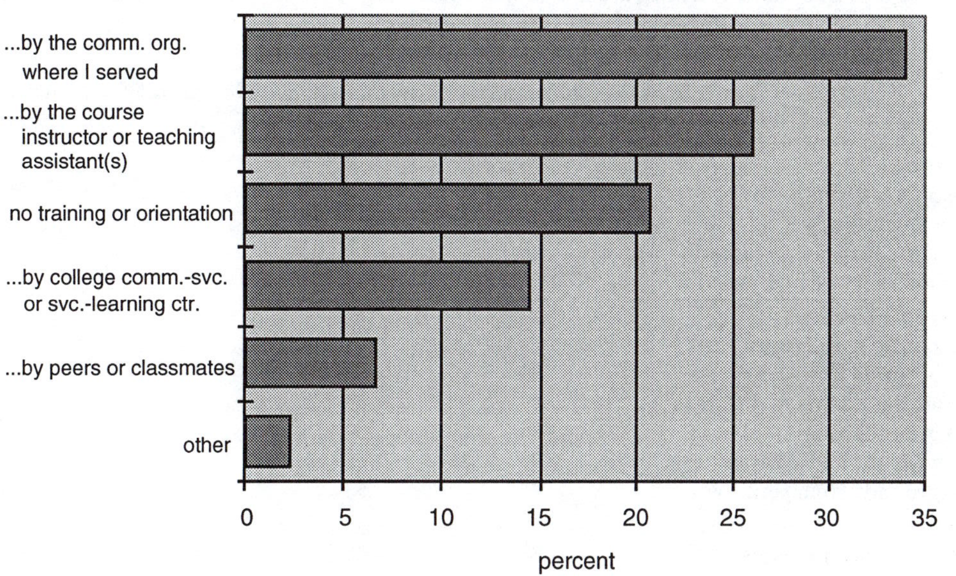

NOTE: Respondents could select more than one response.

Figure 4.4—"What kind of training or orientation did you receive specifically related to your volunteer or community service activities?"

Respondents' community service was supervised by the following: community organization staff (43 percent), course instructor or teaching assistant (38 percent), staff from a college or university community service center (12 percent), or peers or classmates (7 percent). Only 7 percent were unsupervised.

Class Experiences

Service-learning practitioners have emphasized the need for "reflection," or activities that engage students in analyzing their service experiences and connecting service to the content of their course. Thus, the Student Survey asked students to indicate whether they participated in a variety of reflective activities. As shown in Table 4.9, most courses included some form of structured reflection on the service experience, such as writing a paper, keeping a journal, or studying the causes of the social problems their service addressed. Table 4.10 provides additional information about reflection activities. Results are suggestive of periodic, though not frequent, efforts to link course content and community service.

Table 4.9 shows that service-learning courses also provided other kinds of learning opportunities. A majority of students in service-learning courses gained exposure to people of different backgrounds from their own. Courses also promoted teamwork. Only half the courses provided students with career information, although this percentage is higher for community colleges, consistent with their vocational emphasis.

Table 4.9

Percentage of Service-Learning Respondents Who Engaged in Various Activities as Part of Their Course

Activity	Research University	Comp. and Liberal Arts	Community College	Aggregate Sample
Reflection				
Write a paper related to service	73	85	79	79
Keep a journal about service	61	66	59	62
Study the causes of the social problems service addressed	62	64	55	61
Exposure to Diversity				
Serve people of different backgrounds from your own	91	75	77	82
Work with students of different backgrounds from your own	71	60	70	67
Work with staff of different backgrounds from your own	74	54	71	65
Teamwork				
Conduct service in teams	63	68	54	62
Carry out assignments in teams	56	70	62	62
Other				
Learn about different careers	44	47	62	50
Engage in creative or artistic activities	48	47	41	45

Table 4.10

Mean Ratings of How Often Service-Learning Respondents Participated in Various Activities as Part of Their Service-Learning Course

Activity	Research University	Comp. and Liberal Arts	Community College	Aggregate Sample
Apply course concepts to service activities	3.4	3.6	3.4	3.5
Discuss service experiences in class	3.4	3.5	3.3	3.4
Talk with the instructor out of class about service	2.5	2.7	2.8	2.7
Read books or articles related to community service	2.4	2.8	2.3	2.5

NOTE: Ratings were made on five-point scales, with 1 = "never" and 5 = "often."

Satisfaction with the Service-Learning Experience

Service-learning respondents rated their satisfaction with elements of the course using a five-point scale ranging from "very dissatisfied" to "very satisfied." As Table 4.11 shows, respondents rated all the elements above the midpoint of the scale. Although the research university respondents' responses were lower than those of the other two groups, this only reflects the way in which that particular group "grades" and is not indicative of lesser quality in research university service-learning courses.

Table 4.11

Mean Ratings of Respondents' Satisfaction with Service-Learning Course

	Research University	Comp. and Liberal Arts	Comm. College	Aggregate Sample
Opportunities to reflect on your service experience	3.9	4.1	4.2	4.1
The substance of the course	3.9	4.2	4.2	4.1
The quality of instruction	3.8	4.3	4.2	4.1
Your responsibilities and activities as a volunteer	3.7	4.1	4.1	3.9
Opportunities to discuss the service experience in class	3.8	3.9	3.9	3.9
The process by which students were placed in service sites	3.6	3.9	3.9	3.8
Link between service activities and the course content	3.6	3.9	3.9	3.8
Link between service and the learning objectives of the course	3.6	4.0	3.9	3.8
Opportunities to discuss service experiences outside of class	3.7	3.8	3.8	3.8
Feedback about your service activities	3.5	3.8	3.9	3.7
Opportunities for creative expression	3.5	3.9	3.9	3.7
Spirit of community in the class	3.5	3.8	3.9	3.7
Training for your service responsibilities	3.3	3.7	3.6	3.5

Factors That Influence Perceived Outcomes of Service-Learning

The Student Survey results show great variation in service-learning courses. In this section, we systematically examine this variation to identify some of the factors that may affect respondents' service-learning experiences.

We considered four types of factors that might influence students' experiences: (a) demographic characteristics; (b) institutional type; (c) students' volunteer activities, such as the number of hours they served and the sites at which they volunteered; and (d) course structure and activities. We then constructed four sets of multiple linear regression models in order to determine which factors influenced students' service-learning experiences. That is, we regressed each of the four outcome scores (academic skills, professional skills, life skills, and civic participation) on the various categories of possible influencing variables.

We started by specifying a "standard" (i.e., typical) service-learning student. This student was an undergraduate, under 26 years old, and not attending a research university. He or she participated in service as part of the course, volunteered for an educational or health-related organization, and served less than 21 hours over the length of the course. This hypothetical person did not work as part of a team, received some type of supervision and training, and was allowed to choose the organization in which he or she served.

Table 4.12 displays the model results. Our standard student's predicted score for each outcome is indicated in the top row of the table. In each of the rows that follow, we demonstrate how the scores would change if we varied *one characteristic*. For example, the table indicates that the standard student has a predicted academic outcome score of 3.58. A student with all the same characteristics as the standard student, except for being over 25 years of age, would have a predicted academic outcome score of 3.58+0.13=3.71. If this same student had attended a research university, the academic outcome score would be 3.58+0.13-0.10=3.61.[12]

If a characteristic does not produce any incremental change in a given outcome, the cell is left empty. For example, Table 4.12 indicates that there is no difference in the civic outcome area between the standard student and a student with all the same characteristics except age over 25 years. For that matter, there is also no difference in the civic outcome between the standard student and one who attends a research university.

None of the models found gender to be significant. In other words, gender is not a significant predictor for any of the outcome scores *within* the service-learning respondent group (even though it may predict the likelihood of participating in service-learning courses in the first place). This is why the standard student may be either male or female.

We note that the R^2 values for these models are all quite small, ranging from 0.06 for the academic outcome to 0.13 for the professional outcome. This implies that the models do not explain a significant amount of variation, making them of little use for prediction. In other words, many factors other than those included in the analyses presented here affect students' responses to the survey items about course outcomes. Yet for the purposes of this analysis—indicating how various course characteristics affect student's ratings of the course in the four outcome dimensions—the results are useful and provide insight.

Table 4.12 indicates that, relative to the standard student, a student who opted out of participating in service altogether would show more positive outcomes for academic skills and life skills. This is certainly contrary to the expectations of service-learning practitioners and proponents. However, students with certain kinds of service experiences are likely to show even stronger outcomes than are the nonparticipants. For example, the results indicate that students who volunteered for more than 20 hours and applied course constructs to their service experiences would receive an academic skills outcome score of 4.11—0.36 higher than that for the standard student and 0.08 higher than that for the nonparticipant. If the

[12]In the regression models that generated these predictions, the standard errors have been adjusted for the clustering of students within classes.

Table 4.12

How Outcome Scores Are Affected by Various Course and Demographic Factors

	Outcome			
Characteristics	Civic	Life	Academic	Professional
"Standard" Student's Score	3.33	3.75	3.58	3.67
Demographics				
Over 25 years of age			+0.13	+0.19
Attended research university		-0.10	-0.10	-0.20
Graduate student		-0.24		
Teaching student		+0.28		
Student-Related Variables				
Self-selected into course	+0.14	+0.17		+0.13
Volunteered with "other" organization	+0.19	+0.08	+0.11	+0.17
Did not participate in service as part of the course		+0.38	+0.28	
Volunteered for more than 20 hours (over the course)		+0.12	+0.12	
Course-Related Variables				
Applied course concepts to service activities	+0.17	+0.38	+0.24	+0.36
Discussed service experience in class		+0.18		
No training for service	-0.11			
Did not receive any supervision while volunteering				-0.28
Assigned to the volunteer organization				-0.15
Conducted service as part of a team				-0.13

students also discussed their service experiences in class, their life skills outcome score would total 4.43—0.75 higher than that for the standard student and 0.37 higher than that for the nonparticipant.

These results demonstrate that all service-learning courses are not created equal. At worst, opting out of service may be a better choice than participating. Those courses that apply course constructs to students' service experiences are notably stronger. Other beneficial factors include discussing service in class (in the life skills outcome) and providing supervision (in the professional skills outcome). Such findings lend support to those who advocate the inclusion of reflection in service-learning.

It is noteworthy that students who volunteer in any of CNS's four priority areas of service are expected to receive lower scores in all four outcome areas than are students who volunteer in other areas of service. Unfortunately, the majority of service-learning recipients select education and health-related organizations, and a number of initiatives (e.g., America Reads) are promoting greater involvement of college student volunteers in K–12 schools. More research is needed to determine whether this finding holds with other samples; if so, this may carry important implications for service-learning policies and programs.

Student characteristics, too, influence the perceived outcomes of service-learning courses. Students over 25 years of age, for example, show higher scores for academic and professional skills than do their younger peers. More positive outcomes are also associated with those who self-select into service-learning courses, choose somewhat nontraditional service sites, and serve for over 20 hours.

Finally, different approaches may be optimal for different outcomes. For example, the results show that class discussion about service is strongly associated with perceived improvements in life skills but not with other outcome areas of interest. Supervision is associated with perceived improvements in professional development but not with academic skills, life skills, or civic participation.

SUMMARY OF CONCLUSIONS

In spite of the low response rate, our results are fairly consistent across various levels of data aggregation. In particular, most of the aggregate results have corresponded well to the results from the six select schools, which as a group had a reasonably high response rate. Thus, we find some reason to believe that the high nonresponse rate did not bias our aggregate results. On the other hand, we also found evidence that approximately one in four students self-selected into the service-learning courses, which possibly introduces other biases in the results. Thus, consistent with the "quantitative case study" approach, results should not be generalized to the population of college students.

Throughout the analysis, we found that respondents from research universities differed from respondents from community colleges, comprehensive universities, and liberal arts colleges. In particular, service-learning and comparison group respondents within research universities showed fewer demographic differences than did service-learning and comparison group respondents within other types of institutions. Similarly, we found no difference in self-reported GPAs between service-learning and comparison group respondents from research universities, while in other types of institutions, service-learning respondents had higher GPAs than did comparison group respondents. We also found that research university service-learning respondents reported that their courses required more reading and more contact with classmates, while respondents from the other institutional types reported just the opposite. Finally, we found that attending a research university is associated with slightly lower scores in three of the four service-learning outcome areas studied (i.e., in life, academic, and professional skills).

How Do Students in Service-Learning Courses Differ from Other Students?

Relative to the comparison group, the service-learning group included a higher proportion of females and was older. Service-learning students also had slightly higher GPAs. The groups did not differ with regard to race, student and employment status, and degree sought. No evidence was found to support the hypothesis that service-learning students had more prior community service experience.

Are Service-Learning Courses Easier Than Other Courses?

There is little evidence that service-learning courses are less demanding than comparison courses. Results indicated that, relative to comparison courses, the service-learning courses required more writing and more time devoted to the course. In addition, the service-learning students and the comparison students showed no difference in expected course grades.

How Satisfied Are Students with Service-Learning Courses?

Service-learning respondents were more satisfied than the comparison respondents with their courses. About two-thirds of service-learning respondents described their course as "above average" or "one of the best courses I've ever taken," compared to about 55 percent of comparison group respondents.

How Do Respondents Believe That Participation in Service-Learning Affects Their Skills and Development?

A general and fairly strong difference exists between the service-learning and comparison groups in self-reported civic participation, followed by a moderate difference in perceived life skills and no difference in academic or professional skills.

Further examination of the civic participation category revealed that a service-learning experience shows the smallest association with students' perceived current and future political activity, a moderate association with current and future societal problem solving and on-campus political activity, and the strongest association with students' expectations about participating in community service in the future.

Those students who self-selected into service-learning courses also showed effects in the professional skills outcome area, suggesting that self-selectors consider community service to be more closely related to their career aspirations than do other service-learning respondents.

What Is the Level of Respondents' Involvement in Service as Part of Service-Learning Courses? What Is the Nature of Their Involvement?

About one in four respondents reported that they knew about the service component of the course prior to enrolling and wanted to participate in service, suggesting that a substantial minority of respondents self-select into service-learning courses.

About one in five (21 percent) of the service-learning course students did not participate in service. Two-thirds (66 percent) of the nonparticipants reported that they lacked the time to participate. Nonparticipants were more likely to be male and over 21 years of age.

Among those who did participate in service as part of their course, the median volunteering time was 20 hours over the course of the semester or quarter. One-half of these respondents volunteered for educational organizations, and another third volunteered for health-related organizations. The remainder volunteered for other types of organizations, such as legal clinics and environmental agencies.

How Are Community Service Participants Placed, Trained, and Supervised?

Practices varied widely by school. In the aggregate, roughly one-third of the participants selected their volunteer opportunity using information provided by their course instructor; another third were assigned. Over 20 percent used materials provided by community organizations, and about 10 percent selected the organization on their own.

Over 20 percent of participants did not receive any training or orientation for their service activities, but only 7 percent reported that they were untrained. Results suggest that faculty rely heavily on community organizations for training and supervision—staff from community organizations trained about 34 percent of participants and supervised 43 percent. In comparison, faculty or teaching assistants trained about 27 percent and supervised 38 percent.

Do Service-Learning Students Engage in "Reflection," or Structured Analysis of Their Service Experience as It Relates to Their Course?

A majority of the service-learning respondents in all types of institutions participated in some kind of reflection, including writing papers, keeping journals, or analyzing the causes of the social problems their service addressed. Respondents also reported that their courses involved periodic efforts to link the service experience to course content.

Service-learning courses also included other kinds of learning opportunities, particularly exposure to diversity and teamwork.

What Factors Differentiate Service-Learning Courses with Strong Perceived Effects on Student Development from Those with Weaker Effects?

Students who perceived relatively strong effects of service in all four outcome areas (i.e., they received higher scores in all four outcome areas) were more likely than others to report that their course linked the service experience to the course content. They were also more likely to volunteer in organizations other than health care facilities or schools. Those who self-selected into service received higher scores than a "typical" service-learning student in three of the four outcome areas. Those attending research universities received lower scores in three of the four outcome areas.

Other factors had strong effects in one or two outcome areas. For example, relative to "typical" service-learning students, those volunteering for more than 20 hours received higher scores for life and academic skills, and those who did not receive any supervision received lower scores in professional skills.

Students who did not participate in any service received higher scores than a "typical" service-learning student in two of the four outcome areas (with no difference in the other two). However, this negative finding is reversed for students who volunteered more than 20 hours, discussed service experience in class, and enrolled in courses that link course content to service.

The Student Survey results lend partial support to both proponents and opponents of service-learning. On the one hand, there is little evidence that service-learning courses are less rigorous or demanding than other postsecondary courses. Students assess the courses very favorably and perceive the experience as valuable. In addition, there is some evidence that participation in service-learning is associated with an increased commitment to service and enhanced life skills, specifically, understanding of others and interpersonal skills. A very conservative conclusion is that participation in service-learning appears to bring no harm to students and carries some modest positive effects, such as promoting students' satisfaction with their education. A less conservative conclusion is that service-learning may carry stronger benefits for certain students if certain elements are in place, such as links between the course content and service experience.

On the other hand, there is no evidence that service-learning courses are associated with improvements in students' academic abilities or professional preparation, arguably the two primary purposes of higher education. In addition, the increased civic responsibility manifested by service-learning participants in this study is essentially limited to service activities (now and in the future) and does not extend to political involvement.

Data also confirm that some—perhaps many—service-learning participants "self-select" into their courses, suggesting that observed differences between service-learning and comparison respondents may be the result of pre-existing group differences. The results also suggest that those who self-select perceive service-learning as more influential, particularly in the area of professional skills.

These findings are generally consistent with prior research on service-learning, including the Sax, Astin, and Astin (1996) longitudinal survey conducted as part of the LSAHE evaluation. Results of both studies indicate a statistically significant association between participation in service-learning (or service) during college and increased civic skills/participation and life skills. In both cases, effect sizes are small but appear consistently across a wide range of outcome measures, institutional types, and student characteristics. Unlike the results reported here, Sax, Astin, and Astin also found evidence of positive effects of service on academic skills and professional preparation. Many different factors may account for this discrepancy, including differences in the samples, response rates, sample size, instrumentation, and design. Both studies also found that a large proportion of students self-select into service-learning opportunities and that these students differ from those who do not self-select.

Additional research is needed to understand and quantify effects of service-learning on student participants. The existing research, including this study, is generally based on "soft" data comprising self-reported attitudes and behaviors. Furthermore, these studies are subject to many possible biases. To promote a better, more accurate understanding of the effects of service-learning, we recommend that future research include randomized, longitudinal designs. Studies that determine whether service-learning has an effect on student actions, as opposed to beliefs or reported actions, are also needed. These methods will reduce bias in the data and increase the accuracy of results.

5. WHAT WERE LSAHE IMPACTS ON COMMUNITY ORGANIZATIONS?

INTRODUCTION

A key goal of the LSAHE evaluation was to assess the effectiveness of LSAHE-supported programs in strengthening the service sector and meeting community needs. The perceptions of community organization staff (i.e., staff in community-based agencies, government agencies, schools, and health care facilities where students provided volunteer service) are especially important in evaluating LSAHE impacts on communities. The staff regularly observe the work of volunteers and therefore are in the best position to assess their effectiveness. In addition, staff assessments are important to the long-term success of collegiate service programs because such programs depend on cooperation from community organizations. If the difficulties and problems of working with student volunteers outweigh the benefits, community organizations will no longer welcome their participation and the service programs will decline.

RAND therefore surveyed a random sample of community organizations that served as host sites for student volunteers from institutions with LSAHE grants. The survey questionnaire asked community organizations to evaluate the contributions of student volunteers from a designated "partner" college or university that had an LSAHE grant or subgrant and had identified the organization as a site for its student volunteers. More specifically, the questionnaire asked for:

- *Descriptions* of the community organizations involved in LSAHE, student efforts, and the beneficiaries of student service;
- *Assessments* by the community organizations of the student volunteers from their partner college or university, including:
  - (a) the students' effects on the community organization,
  - (b) the students' effects on service recipients, and
  - (c) the strengths and weaknesses of the students as service providers.

Items assessing students' effects on service recipients were designed to articulate with the outputs included in the Accomplishments Survey (which were themselves based on content analysis of grantees' proposals, program descriptions, and plans). Ratings of students' effects on community organizations and their strengths and weaknesses were based on a review of the literature on how to build strong service programs (e.g., Kupiec, 1993; Tice, 1994), as well as on interviews with community organization staff and program directors during early site visits.

The survey was conducted twice, in Fiscal 1995 and Fiscal 1996. In Fiscal 1995, 443 community organizations, or 69 percent of the sample, returned the questionnaire. In Fiscal 1996, 404 organizations responded, representing a 64 percent response rate. Different community organizations were surveyed each year, so there are no longitudinal comparisons.

Because community organization staff found it difficult to distinguish volunteers in LSAHE-supported programs from volunteers in non-LSAHE-supported programs within the same college or university, the Community Impact Survey asked questions in reference to *all* student volunteers from the designated partner institution. This raises the question, then, of whether the results inform LSAHE specifically, or whether they apply only to student volunteers in general.

A number of observations increase our confidence that the results apply to LSAHE. First, recall that LSAHE funds were combined with other funds and used to seed a variety of service initiatives, so there are few if any uniquely identifiable LSAHE participants. Second, consultation with approximately 15 percent of LSAHE program directors (and informal discussion with many more) confirmed that in the vast majority of cases, all or most of the volunteers from a college at any given site were students from LSAHE-supported programs. This was true both when LSAHE-supported programs focused their efforts on a small number of sites (since in such cases they tended to focus on underserved schools and agencies in the community) and when programs dispersed students across a large number of sites (since in such cases coordination was provided by a LSAHE-supported center, as described in Chapter 6).

Although the respondents did not consistently know the programs or courses in which their student volunteers participated, they did know the colleges that their student volunteers attended. In some cases, only the designated partner LSAHE institution sent student volunteers to the site. In other cases, especially those involving large urban schools and preschools, two or more colleges sent volunteers to the site. These cases provided an opportunity to compare the perceived quality of student volunteers from institutions with LSAHE grants to the perceived quality of those from other higher education institutions.

Analyses of the survey data included comparisons based on the standard stratification variables used throughout the study (see Chapter 2), as well as additional variables derived from the Community Impact Survey. None of these stratification variables, however, yielded significant differences, because the ratings are uniformly high and show little variation. Statistical analysis also indicates a high level of intercorrelation among items, so they should not be viewed as independent or distinct constructs, but rather as components of a broader construct of the perceived effectiveness or quality of the student volunteers.

In addition to the Community Impact Survey, the site visits to institutions with LSAHE grants provided information about LSAHE effects on communities. The site visits included interviews with staff from community organizations in which students volunteered and with student volunteers themselves, as well as direct observation of the students performing service. Some site visits also included brief interviews with direct recipients of service. The possible confusion between LSAHE- and non-LSAHE-supported volunteers does not apply to the case studies, since program directors and the students indicated whether the student volunteers we observed were participants in LSAHE-supported programs. (At no site did we observe LSAHE-supported and non-LSAHE volunteers from the same institution in the same community organization, although in a few cases we did observe LSAHE-supported volunteers and volunteers from another college in the same community organization.) The site visit results are highly consistent with the results of the Community Impact Survey.

This chapter discusses how community organizations perceived the impact and effectiveness of student volunteers from institutions with LSAHE grants. The next section describes the organizations with which LSAHE-supported programs worked, the students' level of effort, and the beneficiaries of student service. We then describe community organization assessments of the student volunteers and the benefits and challenges community organizations encountered in working with student volunteers.

DESCRIPTIVE INFORMATION

Characteristics of Community Organizations in the Sample

As shown in Table 5.1, LSAHE-supported programs were most likely to work with private nonprofit organizations or school districts. About half the organizations employed ten or fewer full-time employees. The organizations served about 250 people per month.[1]

Table 5.1

Percentage of Respondents, by Type of Organization

Organization Type	Fiscal 1995	Fiscal 1996
Private nonprofits	49	56
School districts	31	24
Government agencies	12	14
For-profit organizations	2	2
Unspecified	7	4

Of the four areas of community need emphasized in LSAHE legislation—education, health and human services, environment, and public safety—the community organizations responding to the Community Impact Survey were most likely to focus on education and health and least likely to focus on public safety and the environment. This pattern is consistent with findings from the Accomplishments Survey.

[1]Fiscal 1995 survey results indicate a median of 235 individuals served per month, and Fiscal 1996 results indicate a median of 250 per month.

Level of Student Volunteer Activity

In each year, the community organizations reported engaging an average of ten student volunteers from their partner college or university. As Table 5.2 indicates, these students provided each organization with about 300 service hours during the academic year.[2]

Table 5.2

Median Service Hours by Student Volunteers from Institutions with LSAHE Grants

Service Hours	Fiscal 1995 (N=434)	Fiscal 1996 (N=404)
Hours per month of service provided by all volunteers from partner institution	64	50
Total service hours (September through April)	300	301

Service Recipients

Respondents to the Community Impact Survey reported that student volunteers helped about 30 people each month (median of 30 in Fiscal 1995 and 34 in Fiscal 1996). Table 5.3 displays the primary beneficiaries of these services.

Table 5.3

Types of People Served by Student Volunteers from Institutions with LSAHE Grants (Top Five Populations Identified)

	Percentage of Respondents	
Service Beneficiaries	Fiscal 1995 (N=434)	Fiscal 1996 (N=404)
K–12 students	56	57
Economically disadvantaged	47	55
Educationally disadvantaged	39	41
"At-risk" youth	38	38
Families/parents	30	41

NOTE: Percentages sum to over 100 percent because many organizations provided services to more than one type of beneficiary.

Consistent with Accomplishments Survey results, these responses reflect the large emphasis on education and improving student achievement. An average community organization also reported that more than three-quarters (median) of the service recipients assisted by the student volunteers had family incomes at or below the poverty level.

[2]Means are not reported due to their sensitivity to extreme values. One example of an outlier raising the mean, but not the median, is one city recreation department that counted the entire city population of 88,000 as its service recipients.

ASSESSMENT OF STUDENT VOLUNTEERS

The Community Impact Survey asked respondents to evaluate the quality of the services provided by student volunteers from institutions with LSAHE grants. This section discusses five types of evaluative ratings:

1. Student volunteers' strengths and weaknesses as service providers;
2. How student volunteers compared to other service providers;
3. Student volunteers' impacts on community organizations;
4. Student volunteers' impacts on the direct recipients of service;
5. Student volunteers' overall effectiveness.

High intercorrelations among items suggest that these constructs are closely related to one another.

Student Volunteers' Strengths and Weaknesses

The Community Impact Survey results indicate that community organizations perceived student volunteers from their partner institutions as possessing strong interpersonal and work-related skills. As Figure 5.1 demonstrates, students received the highest ratings for "enthusiasm" and the lowest for "skills in the area of service

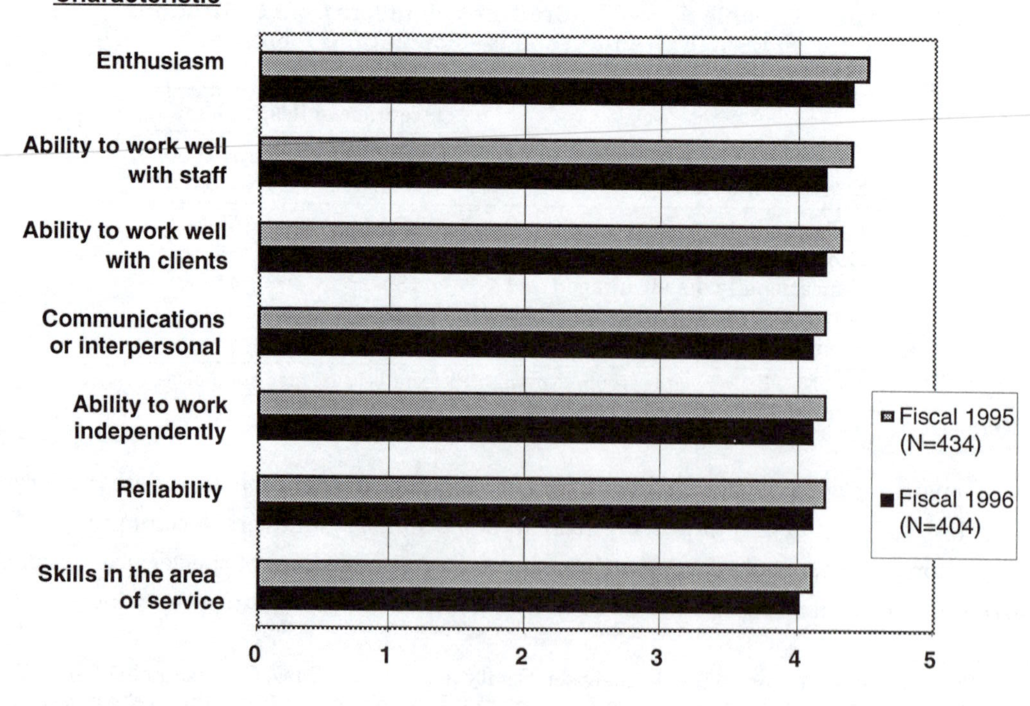

(On a scale from 1 to 5, where 1 = "poor" and 5 = "excellent.")

Figure 5.1—Mean Ratings of Student Volunteer Characteristics

provided." Even the lowest-rated area, however, was still strongly positive and well above the midpoint of the scale.

Comparison with Other Service Providers

To place the strengths and weaknesses of student volunteers from institutions with LSAHE grants in context, Community Impact Survey respondents were asked to compare them to other volunteers and to paid service providers.

Survey results shown in Figure 5.2 reveal that more than half the respondents considered student volunteers from their partner institution to be more effective than other volunteers and about equal in effectiveness to paid staff. These students also exceeded respondents' expectations.

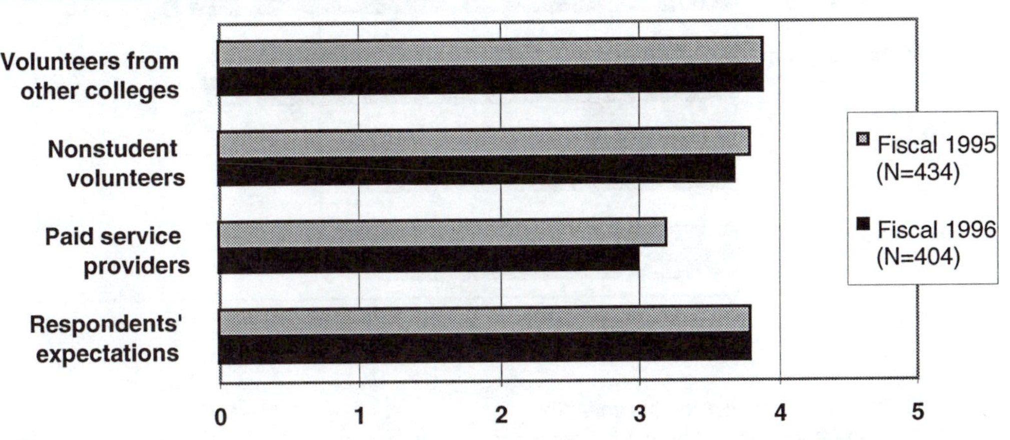

(On a scale from 1 to 5, where 1 = "much worse than others," 3 = "about the same," and 5 = "much better than others.")

Figure 5.2—Mean Ratings of Student Volunteers from Institutions with LSAHE Grants

Impact on Community Organizations

To determine whether student volunteers from institutions with LSAHE grants enhanced the community organizations in which they served, a series of survey questions asked respondents to evaluate the impact of the volunteers on their organization's activities or services. As Figure 5.3 demonstrates, students received highly positive ratings both years. The Fiscal 1996 survey included a new item about student volunteers' impact on staff morale, which also received positive ratings.

In both years, the statements regarding impact on number and workload of paid staff received the lowest mean scores. These ratings suggest that student volunteers had essentially no impact on the number and workload of paid staff.

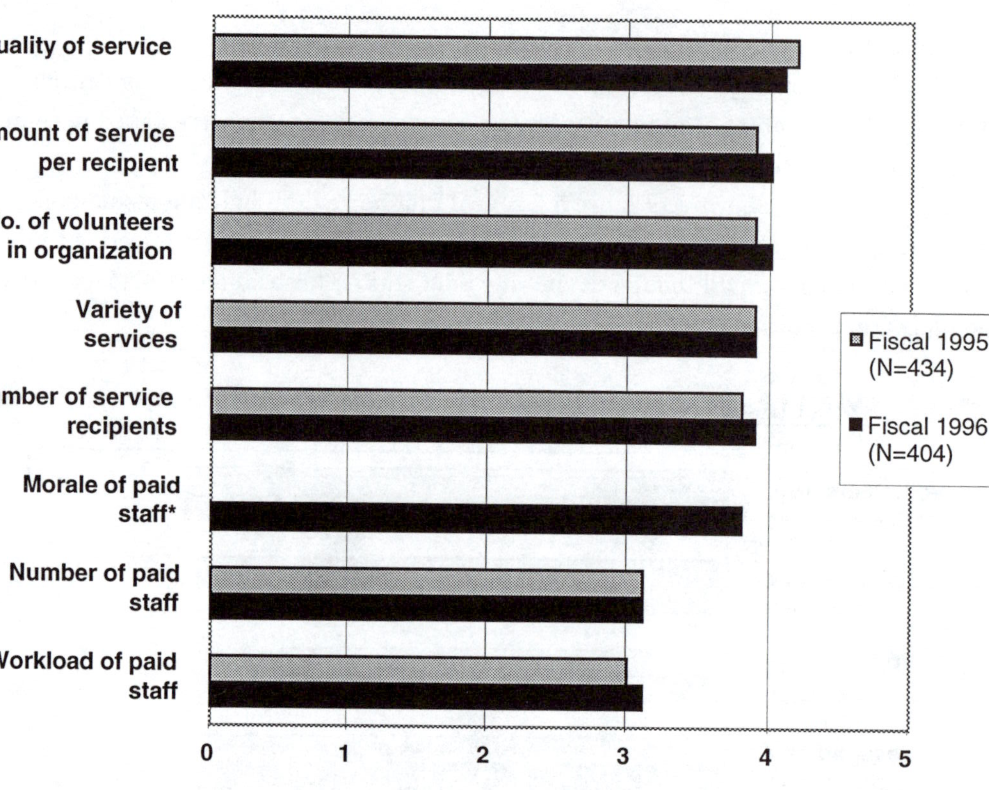

*1995 data not available for this variable.

(On a scale from 1 to 5, where 1 indicates that volunteers' efforts led to a decrease or decline on the dimension, 3 indicates that the volunteers' efforts had no effect, and 5 indicates that volunteers' efforts led to improvements or increases on the dimension.)

Figure 5.3—Mean Ratings of How Student Volunteers Affected Community Organizations' Activities and Services

Impact on Direct Recipients of Service

Respondents to the Community Impact Survey also rated the effectiveness of student volunteers from their partner institutions in the four areas of service: education, health and human needs, environment, and public safety. As Figures 5.4 through 5.7 indicate, all of the items yielded ratings well above the midpoint of the scale, and the overall means varied only slightly for the two years. The responses also reflect the diversity of volunteer activities and responsibilities in the four areas of service.

Site visit observations provided additional insights into the ways in which student volunteers worked with service recipients. For example:

- In the area of education, RAND observed students tutoring low-achieving elementary school students, focusing their assistance on math, reading, and computer skills. The teachers attributed measurable gains in children's test

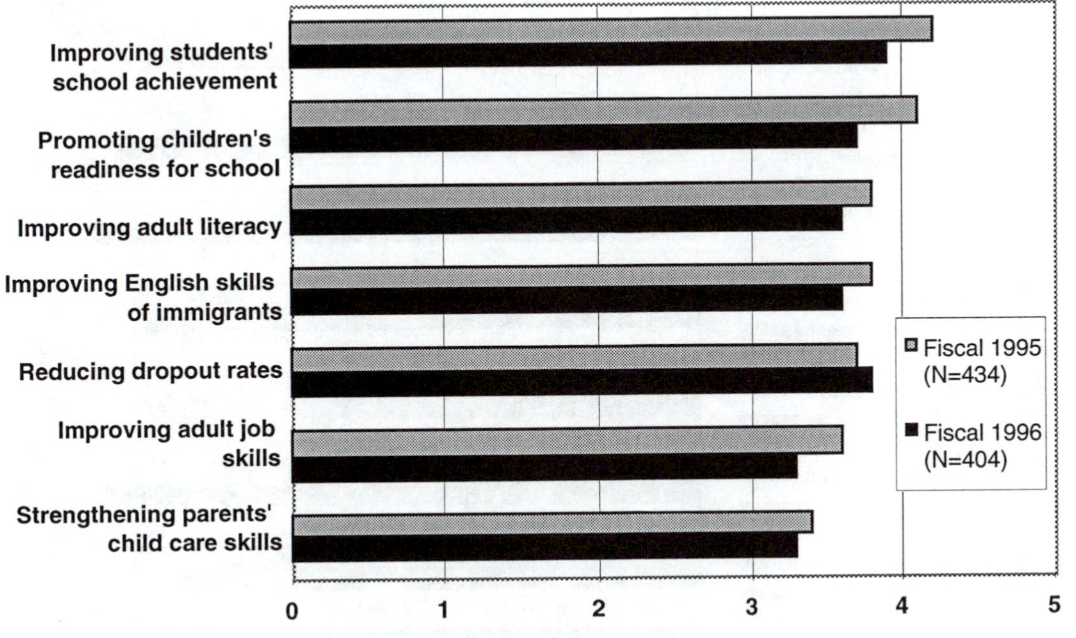

(On a scale from 1 to 5, where 1 = "not effective" and 5 = "highly effective." Base = Respondents engaging student volunteers in service in education.)

Figure 5.4—Mean Ratings by Community Organizations of Student Volunteers' Effectiveness in Providing Educational Services

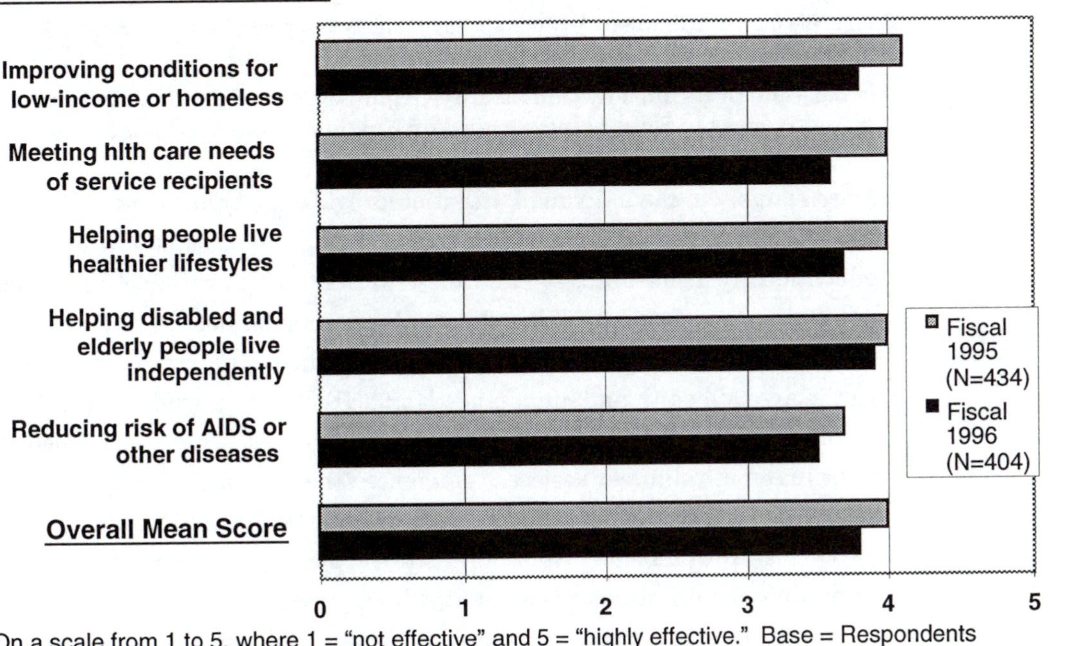

(On a scale from 1 to 5, where 1 = "not effective" and 5 = "highly effective." Base = Respondents engaging student volunteers in service in health and human needs.)

Figure 5.5—Mean Ratings by Community Organizations of Student Volunteers' Effectiveness in Providing Health and Human Needs Services

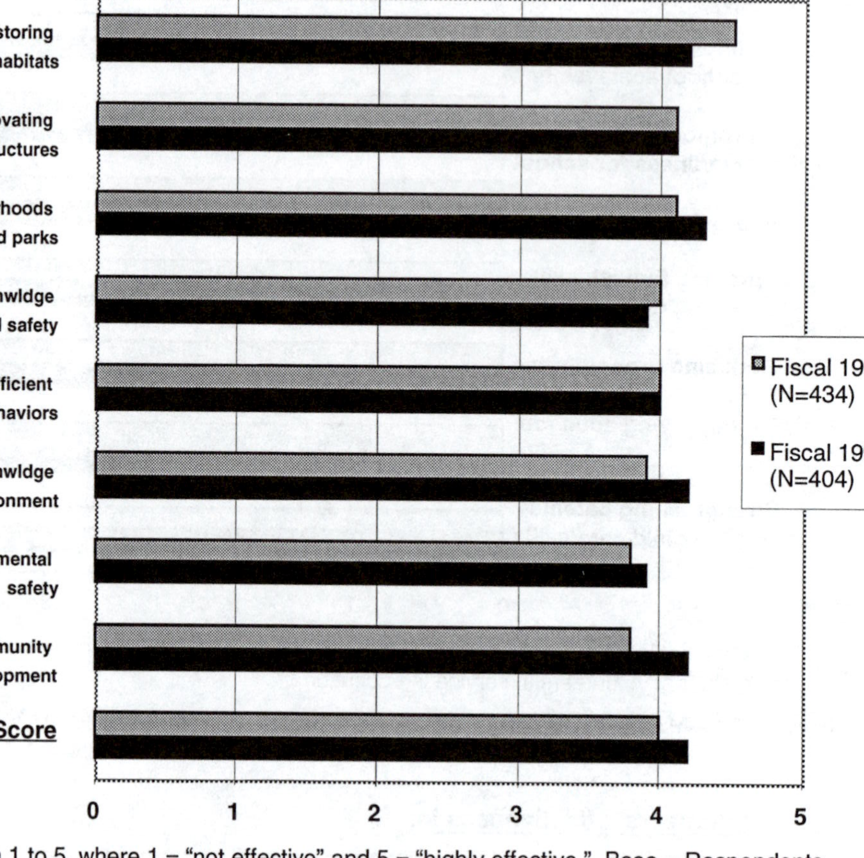

(On a scale from 1 to 5, where 1 = "not effective" and 5 = "highly effective." Base = Respondents engaging student volunteers in service to the environment.)

Figure 5.6 —Mean Ratings by Community Organizations of Student Volunteers' Effectiveness in Enhancing Natural or Neighborhood Environments

scores largely to the individual attention provided by volunteers. At another site, student volunteers staffed an after-school center and assisted low-income and educationally disadvantaged children with their homework. School personnel noted that because many of the children's parents did not speak English and could not help their children with schoolwork, the volunteers' help was essential.

- In the area of health and human needs, RAND observed students conducting oral histories with members of a senior center in an inner-city neighborhood. The coordinator of volunteer services commented that the opportunity for seniors to share their personal and cultural traditions had positive effects on their psychological well-being. At another site, medical students conducted a community health needs assessment, which provided the foundation for health planning. At still another site, students taught children of migrant farm workers to swim, thereby helping to prevent drowning, the most common cause of death for migrant children in the community.

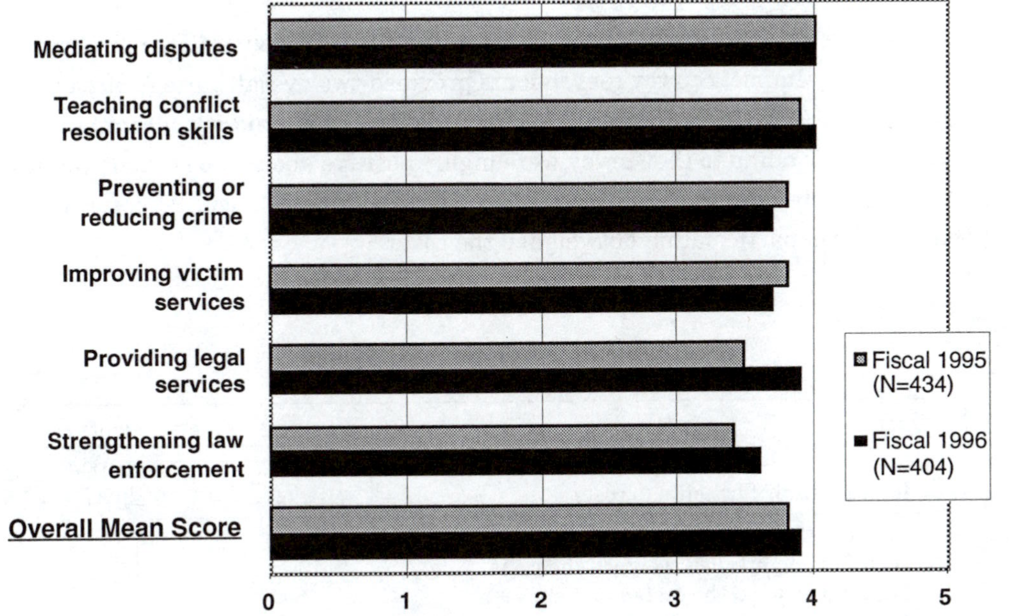

(On a scale from 1 to 5, where 1 = "not effective" and 5 = "highly effective." Base = Respondents engaging student volunteers in service in public safety.)

Figure 5.7—Mean Ratings by Community Organizations of Student Volunteers' Effectiveness in Providing Public Safety and Legal Services

- In the area of environment, RAND observed students working with an urban after-school program to determine the lead content in soil on the elementary school grounds. Student volunteers discussed the health hazards of lead exposure and worked with elementary school students to collect samples with teaspoons and jars. Samples were brought back to the LSAHE institution for analysis. By raising children's awareness of environmental hazards, the volunteers helped to prevent lead poisoning in these children and their siblings according to the staff; additionally, the test results could spur interventions to reduce lead content of the soil.
- In the area of public safety, RAND observed students visiting young men in a residential facility for juvenile offenders. Center staff noted that students modeled appropriate social behavior, encouraged the residents to continue their education, and reassured them that society had not forgotten them. For a similar program, students pursuing substance abuse counseling and law enforcement degrees staffed a juvenile delinquency program, counseling juvenile delinquents and supervising community service activities performed by the youths. At other sites, conflict mediation services provided by law and prelaw students were

viewed as important improvements in the learning environment within various middle and high schools.

Overall Ratings of Student Volunteers from Institutions with LSAHE Grants

Community Impact Survey respondents provided two overall ratings of student volunteers. The results for both years indicated that the vast majority of community organizations responding to the survey were highly positive about the student volunteers from their designated partner institution. As shown in Table 5.4, over 90 percent believed that the benefits of participation outweighed the costs.

Table 5.4

Benefits Compared to Costs

	Percentage of Respondents	
Relationship of benefits to costs	Fiscal 1995 (N=434)	Fiscal 1996 (N=404)
Benefits "far" outweighed the costs	76	75
Benefits "slightly" outweighed the costs	16	15
Benefits equaled the costs/problems	6	7
Costs outweighed the benefits	2	3

To obtain another overall opinion of the program, respondents were asked, If you had it to do over again, would you still use (college) student volunteers? In Fiscal 1995, nearly every respondent (97 percent) said yes, the remaining 3 percent were unsure, and *no one* said no. The Fiscal 1996 results were also extremely positive: 94 percent said yes, 3 percent were unsure, and 4 percent said no.

BENEFITS AND CHALLENGES IN WORKING WITH HIGHER EDUCATION INSTITUTIONS

Community Impact Survey Results

In addition to providing numerical ratings, respondents were invited to comment on the most significant benefits their organization obtained from working with their designated partner college or university, and the challenges or problems the organization experienced. Results for Fiscal 1996 were grouped into categories for analysis.

As shown in Table 5.5, nearly one-third (29 percent) of community organization respondents described student volunteers as good role models, and 28 percent noted that the volunteers enabled the community organization to provide more services and/or serve more people. Community organization staff interviewed during RAND site visits reiterated these opinions.

At the same time, respondents listed areas for improvement, as shown in Table 5.6. In both years, scheduling and transportation were frequently cited problems. The site visits

Table 5.5

Most Significant Benefits Community Organizations Derived from Working with Student Volunteers

Benefits	Percentage of Respondents
Volunteers are role models or provide intergenerational benefits	29
Organization can provide more services or reach more people	28
Volunteers increase awareness of and support for the community organization (by community members, students, and the LSAHE institution)	22
Volunteers provide a high quality product/service	21
Volunteers bring energy and enthusiasm	11

NOTES: Percentages sum to over 100 percent because many respondents listed more than one benefit. Results are based on the 1996 Community Impact Survey.

Table 5.6

Respondent Concerns About Working with Student Volunteers

Concerns and Suggestions for Improvement	Percentage of Respondents
Increase number of students	21
Improve scheduling and transportation	19
Improve communication with partner college	17
Greater institutionalization of whole program	12
Improve students' sense of commitment	9
Improve communication with the students	8
Increase awareness of the program within the community/institution	7
Hire students with specific expertise	4
Other	22

NOTES: Percentages sum to over 100 percent because many respondents listed more than one concern. Results are based on the 1996 Community Impact Survey.

also found that these issues were among the major concerns of community organization staff. Unfortunately, these issues may be inherent in the relationship. For example, academic calendars place constraints on student availability, and many colleges are located far from the service site(s).

Other respondent concerns, however, such as a desire for improved communication with the partner college or greater institutionalization of the service program, may be more easily addressed by higher education institutions. Similarly, additional training and supervision at the college might address the organizations' concerns about the students' sense of commitment.

The most frequently expressed concern, mentioned by 21 percent of respondents, was that more students should have a role in supporting the community organization and assisting service recipients. This "back-handed compliment" speaks to the community organization respondents' overall satisfaction with student volunteers.

Site Visit Results

The site visits supplemented these responses by pointing to factors that facilitate a strong relationship between community organizations and higher education institutions with LSAHE programs. These include:

- *A reliable, committed contact person at both the higher education institution and the community organization.* Staff from many community organizations visited mentioned that the presence of a full-time staff member at the college or university responsible for coordination of the service program was a key contribution to program success. Similarly, LSAHE program directors found that community relations were enhanced when the community organizations had an easily accessible volunteer coordinator.
- *Addressing scheduling issues.* Many community organization staff expressed concern about the short time students serve, often just one semester or quarter. This may limit a student volunteer's ability to build a strong relationship and secure the trust of service recipients. It also can create disconnects with organization needs. For example, postsecondary students may be on summer vacation when high school students need tutoring to prepare for final exams.
- *Clearly stated, realistic expectations of student volunteer and community organization responsibilities.* In addition to being clear, expectations must be appropriate for the students' time commitments and skill levels. Some community organization staff were disappointed that the student volunteers could not provide more time to the agency or did not call in if they were unable to attend. Some LSAHE program directors were disappointed that the community organization did not monitor or supervise student volunteers, plan tasks or projects for them to conduct, or inform the volunteers of relevant events or organizational changes.
- *Connecting students to community organizations as quickly as possible.* Several community organization directors interviewed during site visits cited the time lag in placing students as an obstacle to success due to the already short service cycle provided by student volunteers. An established organizational structure and procedures to match students and service sites helped shorten this lag at a number of sites.
- *Ensuring that placements benefit the community agency and provide meaningful work for students.* This objective can be especially challenging given the limited amount of time many students can devote to community service. Many LSAHE program directors had encountered community organizations that wanted student volunteers to provide clerical or back-office support rather than direct service to clients. Some community organization staff were reluctant to place students in direct service roles given their brief term of service.
- *Addressing transportation issues.* A lack of adequate transportation sometimes meant limiting service sites to those on bus lines or near campus. Some

programs used their limited resources to buy vans or pay for transportation to service sites. Transportation problems were frequently cited as an obstacle to students' reliable attendance.

SUMMARY OF CONCLUSIONS

The community organizations participating in both years of the Community Impact Survey were a diverse group encompassing a wide array of services and service recipients. Both years, about half the group were private nonprofit enterprises, and about one-third were part of a school district.

Respondents to the Community Impact Surveys assigned the student volunteers from their partner institutions high marks on all the dimensions addressed in the survey. The students were especially praised for their enthusiasm and interpersonal skills. Respondents reported that these student volunteers helped community organizations reach more people and improve the quality of services. The student volunteers were also perceived as making important contributions in the four major areas of service—education, health, environment, and public safety.

Respondents rated the student volunteers from their partner institutions as better than other volunteers and about equal in effectiveness to paid staff. Nine out of ten respondents reported that the benefits of working with student volunteers outweighed the disadvantages.

Despite the positive responses, open-ended comments point to some problem areas that should be explored. These include scheduling, transportation, training, and communications between community organizations and higher education institutions. Since many of these issues are difficult to resolve, it is important for community organizations and colleges or universities to work together to develop realistic expectations and goals.

In sum, the Community Impact Survey reveals that community organizations are very satisfied with the contributions of volunteers enrolled in institutions that receive LSAHE support. Even if we assume that nonrespondents to the survey would have been more negative in their evaluations than respondents were, the results would still provide a positive evaluation of the services provided by students in institutions with LSAHE grants. Although many LSAHE-supported programs assign a higher priority to promoting student growth and learning than to serving community needs, clearly community organization staff believe the latter is occurring. This bodes well for the future of service-learning since community support is essential to the long-term success and stability of these programs.

6. HOW DID LSAHE AFFECT HIGHER EDUCATION INSTITUTIONS?

INTRODUCTION

In addition to seeking to serve communities and promote student development, LSAHE sought to strengthen higher education institutions. CNS identified four institutional objectives for LSAHE:

- To expand service opportunities for students;
- To integrate service into course work;
- To promote program sustainment;
- To foster mutually beneficial relationships with community organizations.[1]

The LSAHE evaluation set out to address two questions about these objectives. First, we determined the degree to which these objectives were achieved. Second, we identified cross-cutting factors that facilitated or hindered grantees' ability to achieve the institutional objectives.

We used three methods to address these questions. The Annual Accomplishments Survey provides information about the level and scope of institutional support for service-learning within colleges and universities that received LSAHE grants, subgrants, or subsubgrants. The Community Impact Survey assesses the quality of campus-community relations. The results of these two surveys were used to assess the degree to which the objectives were achieved. In addition, in-depth site visits to 18 LSAHE single institution direct grantees were used to explore the variety of approaches campuses use to meet their objectives and to observe factors that appear to either facilitate or impede their progress.[2]

The remainder of this chapter presents findings related to each of the four institutional objectives. First, we use survey results to indicate the extent to which each objective was achieved. We then use the site visit findings to describe the models used to achieve the objectives and to discuss the barriers to success.

WERE THE OBJECTIVES ACHIEVED?

This section addresses the extent to which institutions receiving LSAHE grants achieved the four objectives described above. The major source of information for this analysis was the Accomplishments Survey, which collected information on (a) the types of support respondents' institutions provided for service-learning and community service, and

---

[1]See, for example, the LSAHE program summary booklet (CNS, 1994).

[2]The project included a total of 30 site visits, but site visits to seven consortia and five AmeriCorps demonstration programs were not included in the analysis discussed in this chapter.

(b) *when* various institutional supports were first introduced. Those introduced prior to Fiscal 1994 predate the LSAHE program, meaning that LSAHE did not generate these forms of support. Those introduced during or after Fiscal 1994 are temporally associated with LSAHE, although we cannot conclude on this basis alone that LSAHE *caused* the change.[3] We therefore use other findings to supplement the Accomplishments data, including results from the Community Impact Survey and site visits.

Accomplishments Survey results are presented for Fiscal 1996 and Fiscal 1997.[4] Within each dataset, we compared responses based on the standard stratification variables. These comparative results are presented only when they achieved statistical significance.

Expanding Service Opportunities for Students

CNS expected LSAHE to increase the number and variety of opportunities for students to participate in service. The most important strategy institutions used to achieve this objective was to integrate service into courses, as discussed in the next section. Our early site visits pointed to a variety of other strategies that institutions used to achieve this objective; these became the basis for the series of questions in the Annual Accomplishments Survey (see Table 6.1).

Table 6.1

Service Opportunities for Students Provided by Institutions Responding to the Accomplishments Survey

	Fiscal 1996		Fiscal 1997	
Type of Support	% of Institutions with Support	% of Those That Began in 1994 or Later[a]	% of Institutions with Support	% of Those That Began in 1994 or Later[a]
Offer curricular and co-curricular service	90	28	95	39
Offer rewards or recognition for participation in service	75	48	66	59
House a service "center" on campus	66	39	not available	not available
Include service activities in orientation	42	59	51	67
Require service to graduate	11	59	11	52

[a]Base = Those institutions offering the support.

[3]Note that all responding institutions were included in this analysis regardless of whether they were in their first, second, or third year of funding. LSAHE had high visibility throughout the higher education sector and may well have influenced institutions that were not grant recipients. In addition, given the slow pace of change in higher education, it is unlikely that all institutional changes could be accomplished during the immediate funding period. Many forms of institutional support may not be implemented until after LSAHE grants terminate, even if LSAHE funding contributed to the impetus for change.

[4]Fiscal 1995 results are not presented here, because different questions were included on the survey instrument.

Results indicate that a majority of institutions responding to the Accomplishments Survey have implemented strategies to provide students with a wide range of service opportunities. Almost all offer both curricular and co-curricular service opportunities, and most house "centers" to facilitate student access to service. Very few, however, require service as a condition of graduation.

Some differences emerged as a function of institutional type. Only 52 percent of community colleges compared to three-quarters of all others house service centers. Liberal arts institutions were most likely to require service as a condition of graduation, while community colleges were least likely to do so (18 percent of liberal arts institutions and no community colleges responding in Fiscal 1997).

Despite some inconsistencies in response patterns between the 1996 and 1997 Accomplishments Surveys, about half of the responding institutions that included service in orientation, offered rewards or recognition for service participation, or required service for graduation began doing so during or after the initiation of the LSAHE program.

Annual Accomplishments results also reveal increases in the number of students participating in LSAHE-supported service programs. Between Fiscal 1996 and Fiscal 1997, participation in LSAHE-supported co-curricular programs increased from 22,894 to 26,092, and participation in LSAHE-supported academic programs increased from 33,174 to 40,133. Although such figures are consistent with the objective of expanding student access to service, they are inconclusive in part because data about student participation in non-LSAHE service programs are unavailable.

Integrating Service into Course Work

CNS encouraged LSAHE grantees to develop service-learning courses, either by developing new courses or adding service to existing courses. The emphasis on course-based service-learning was particularly strong in LSAHE's second and third years.

Evaluation results indicate that almost all LSAHE grantees achieved this objective. Although, as shown in Table 6.1, most grantees offered some service-learning courses before LSAHE began, the grants were used largely to expand the number of such courses. Over three-quarters of all respondents used their LSAHE grants to establish service-learning courses (79 percent of Fiscal 1996 respondents and 86 percent of Fiscal 1997 respondents). Respondents developed an average of three new service-learning courses each year, summing to almost 3,000 new courses between Fiscal 1995 and Fiscal 1997 (see Table 6.2).

Table 6.2

Number of New Service-Learning Courses

Fiscal 1995	Fiscal 1996	Fiscal 1997	Total
1,035	1,150	725	2,910

Table 6.3 displays additional information about the integration of service into academic courses and curricula. These results indicate that institutions with LSAHE grants

were engaged in a variety of efforts to integrate service into the curriculum, and at many institutions, these efforts were temporally linked to the LSAHE program. Nonetheless, the table also shows considerable room for development. For example, fewer than half the respondents reported that their institutions include service in their core curriculum, suggesting that service-learning courses are not fully integrated into academic programs.

Table 6.3

Integration of Service into Courses and Curricula by Institutions Responding to the Accomplishments Survey

	Fiscal 1996		Fiscal 1997	
Types of Support	% of Institutions with Support	% of Those That Began in 1994 or Later[a]	% of Institutions with Support	% of Those That Began in 1994 or Later[a]
Offer service-learning courses in three or more departments	75	54	76	68
Sponsor a faculty committee on service-learning	52	74	63	80
Offer course development funds to faculty	43	67	54	82
Include service-learning in the core curriculum	34	60	43	72

[a]Base = Those institutions offering the support.

These findings are consistent with results from the site visits. Although all of the grantees we visited offered at least one course involving service, service-learning occupied an ancillary or marginal status in many institutions. For example:

- With support from its LSAHE grant, a comprehensive university gained approval from the faculty senate to offer the institution's first service-learning course. Despite this major step, the course reached only a small number of students and was taught by a non-tenure-track instructor.
- A research university with a strong tradition of co-curricular service programs used its LSAHE grant to promote curricular integration of service. Despite some progress, few tenured or tenure-track faculty expressed interest in participating, and at the outset, most service-learning courses were electives taught by graduate students.

At other institutions, however, service-learning did become more integrated into the curriculum. For example, an influential faculty member was highly effective in promoting service-learning within one community college, which more than doubled the number of service-learning courses, many taught by tenured faculty. Similarly, a faculty member at a historically black institution led a successful effort to introduce at least one service-learning course into the curriculum for each major. Many of these courses were taught by senior faculty. Although such success stories indicate that strong curricular integration is possible, they stand out as exceptions to the modal pattern.

Promoting Program Sustainment

An important determinant of LSAHE success is whether grantees are able to sustain their service-learning programs after LSAHE funds terminate. Although the evaluation could not directly address this question, because data were collected before the grants ended, we did ask about some *indicators* of sustainability. More specifically, we determined the percentage of programs with dedicated staff and permanent budget allocations from their institutions, since these resources indicate institutional commitment to the program.

Table 6.4 indicates that roughly half the respondents to the Accomplishments Survey in each year worked in institutions with a sustainable service infrastructure. Comparisons between direct grantees and subgrantees indicate that direct grantees are more likely than subgrantees to have a sustainable infrastructure. For example, the 1997 Accomplishments data indicate that 73 percent of direct grantees had at least one full-time staff person for service-learning programs, and 61 percent had permanent funding. In contrast, only 40 percent of subgrantees and subsubgrantees had full-time staff, and only 38 percent had permanent funding. Similar results emerged from the 1996 Accomplishments Survey.

Table 6.4

Support to Sustain Service-Learning by Institutions Responding to the Accomplishments Survey

	Fiscal 1996		Fiscal 1997	
Types of Support	% of Institutions with Support	% of Those That Began in 1994 or Later[a]	% of Institutions with Support	% of Those That Began in 1994 or Later[a]
At least one staff or faculty member coordinating service programs full-time	51	54	49	59
Permanent funding for service programs	42	33	45	57

[a]Base = Those institutions offering the support.

In addition, research and comprehensive universities were more likely than liberal arts or community colleges to have full-time staff and permanent funding. The 1997 Accomplishments Survey data indicate that 70 percent of research universities, 52 percent of comprehensive universities, 27 percent of community colleges, and 26 percent of liberal arts colleges in the sample had one or more full-time staff for service programs. Similarly, 55 percent of research universities, 45 percent of comprehensive universities, 35 percent of liberal arts colleges, and only 30 percent of community colleges had permanent funding for service-learning. The 1996 Accomplishments Survey revealed similar findings.

Accomplishments data reported in Chapter 3 indicate that many grantees were confident that their institutions would sustain service-learning courses. For example, over two-thirds (71 percent) of respondents to the Fiscal 1997 Accomplishments Survey reported that their institutions would offer some or all of their newly developed service-learning courses the following year. Over a longer time horizon, however, service-learning offerings may erode, particularly in institutions that lack the resources to support and assist faculty in implementing service-learning.

Additional information about sustainability emerges from the Accomplishments Survey results shown in Table 6.5. Slightly over half of the programs had a regular yearly budget allocation, and no more than 10 percent had endowment support. About two-thirds relied on temporary money beyond the LSAHE grant, including grants from funders other than CNS and occasional budget allocations from their institutions. Community colleges and subgrantees were less likely than other respondents to have regular yearly budget allocations.

Table 6.5

Percentage of Accomplishments Survey Respondents Using Various Sources of Funds for Community Service Activities

Source of Support	Fiscal 1996	Fiscal 1997
Other grants	65	63
A regular yearly budget allocation	57	55
One-time or occasional budget allocation	30	28
Revenue generating activities	16	15
Fees or dues	11	13
Endowment	10	7

A review of 27 institutions that were studied in depth for our analysis of return on investment indicates that about 15 percent of the average direct grant was replaced by other types of funding between the second and the third grant year (see Chapter 7 for a more detailed discussion). More time is needed to determine whether institutions are able to fully replace their LSAHE grants with other funds. It is also possible that they can sustain their programs on reduced funding.

Relative to the survey results, the site visits offered a more optimistic forecast. Almost all of the program directors interviewed reported that their programs would continue beyond the funding period, although they might diminish in size or scope. Program directors generally hoped to obtain new grants or to obtain increased institutional support. In some cases, LSAHE-supported programs arranged to share space and other resources with complementary programs after the grant terminated. In other cases, the programs expected to eliminate some activities, such as incentive grants for faculty, while maintaining a core set of service activities. These optimistic forecasts perhaps reflect the deep commitment to service-learning among many of the program directors. Many ran service programs on a shoestring prior to LSAHE and perhaps are prepared to do so again if necessary.

In summary, different data yield different results with regard to sustainability. While the Accomplishments Survey underscores the programs' dependence on temporary and other "soft" funds, the analysis of return on investment indicates that programs have the capacity to replace at least some of their LSAHE funds. The program directors themselves are the most confident of their ability to sustain their programs. For them, the issue is not *whether* the programs will continue but *how* and at what level. Ultimately, follow-up data collection is needed to determine the extent to which the programs and courses introduced with LSAHE support continue beyond the funding period.

Fostering Mutually Beneficial Relationships with Community Organizations

A final institutional objective for LSAHE was to enhance relations between higher education and community organizations. The Annual Accomplishments Survey provides a higher education perspective on whether this objective was achieved, while the Community Impact Survey provides a community perspective.

While community organizations serve as hosts for student volunteers, many higher education institutions also seek to involve these organizations in developing and implementing service programs. The site visits identified two common strategies used by higher education institutions: (1) including community organization staff in planning service programs, and (2) asking community organization staff to visit service-learning classes and discuss the work of their agencies. As shown in Table 6.6, a majority of Accomplishments Survey respondents involved community agencies in both these ways. The data also indicate that roughly half the institutions had been engaged in such activities prior to the LSAHE program.

Table 6.6

Community Involvement in Designing and Implementing Service-Learning, by Institutions Responding to the Accomplishments Survey

	Fiscal 1996		Fiscal 1997	
Types of Involvement	% of Institutions with Support	% of Those That Began in 1994 or Later[a]	% of Institutions with Support	% of Those That Began in 1994 or Later[a]
Include community agencies in planning service activities	83	47	80	59
Invite community agency staff to make in-class presentations	76	56	80	67

[a]Base = Those institutions offering the support.

The extent to which institutions invested in partnerships with community organizations varied as a function of institutional characteristics. The 1996 and 1997 Accomplishments Surveys both indicate that direct grantees were more likely than subgrantees or subsubgrantees to include community agencies in planning. In addition, research universities and community colleges were more likely than comprehensive universities or liberal arts colleges to include community agencies in planning.

While the Accomplishments Survey addresses campus-community relations from the campus point of view, the Community Impact Survey offers a community perspective.

Community agency staff described how the LSAHE program had affected their relations with their partner academic institutions. As shown in Table 6.7, close to half the responding organizations reported increased contact and collaboration with their partner institution after inception of the LSAHE program. (Most others reported no change in the relationship, with no more than 5 percent reporting any deterioration in the relationship.)

Table 6.7

Percentage of Community Impact Survey Respondents Reporting Contacts Between LSAHE-Supported Colleges and Community Organizations

	Fiscal 1995	Fiscal 1996
Use of faculty and staff as consultants to community organizations	52	49
Participation on committees with both community and campus representation	47	45
Number of joint service projects with community organizations	46	56
Use of community organization staff as instructors or consultants on campus	42	44

NOTE: Percentage selecting 4 or 5 on a five-point scale (1=decreased, 3=stayed the same, 5=increased).

WHAT FACTORS PROMOTE OR INHIBIT SUCCESS?

Our results indicate that most institutions with LSAHE grants achieved at least three out of the four institutional objectives. They expanded service opportunities for students, integrated service into course work, and enhanced community relations. It is still too early to determine whether the objective of sustainability has been achieved.

Beyond simply counting the numbers of institutions with various types of support for service-learning, it is important to understand why some institutions were more successful than others in achieving the LSAHE institutional objectives. The site visit component of the evaluation therefore was designed to identify the factors that facilitate or hinder the development of the institutional support needed for success.

Researchers conducted 30 site visits over the three-year evaluation period. Each site visit included interviews with program staff, students, faculty, administrators, and community organization staff. Visits also included direct observation both on campus and in the community. Site visit teams examined the organizational structure of LSAHE-supported programs, their leadership and staffing, programmatic activities, fiscal well-being, and history. Our analysis was based on a subset of 18 site visits to single-institution direct grantees. The other site visits were conducted at consortium hubs or AmeriCorps demonstration programs, which had very different fiscal and organizational relations to higher education institutions and thus produced results that are not applicable to this discussion.

The site visit results point to four factors of critical importance to an institution's ability to achieve sustainable, high quality service-learning programs:

- Service centers;
- Faculty involvement;
- Leadership support;
- A service tradition.

Each of these factors promotes an institution's ability to expand service opportunities, integrate service into courses, sustain service programs, and establish mutually beneficial community relations. Similarly, the absence of these factors creates significant obstacles to success. Each of these cross-cutting factors is discussed below.

Service Centers

The site visits revealed that institutions with one or more units charged with developing and administering service programs—referred to here as *service centers*—were better able to expand and sustain their programs and also had stronger quality controls. Service centers perform a wide variety of functions, including:

- Identifying community agencies interested in student volunteers and assisting them in recruiting and managing volunteers;
- Encouraging faculty to integrate service into their courses, providing technical assistance in course development, and assisting in the administration of service-learning courses by placing, training, and monitoring students;
- Encouraging students to participate in service and providing information about volunteer opportunities;
- Providing students with leadership training and experience by involving students in running the center or helping them develop new service programs;
- Coordinating service activities throughout the campus;
- Maintaining databases of volunteer service opportunities.

The site visits revealed two predominant types of service centers: comprehensive centers, which combine co-curricular and curricular service programs, and bifurcated centers, which separate the two. Over three-quarters of the 18 sites included in our analysis had centers, slightly more than the LSAHE grantee population as a whole. Eight sites had comprehensive centers, five had bifurcated centers, one had a community service center only, and four did not have any LSAHE-supported centers.

Institutions without centers are hindered in their efforts to develop service-learning since a larger burden falls on faculty. Without the support of a center, faculty teaching service-learning courses must locate sites, place students, coordinate scheduling and transportation, manage site relations, and monitor student attendance and performance on site. Few faculty have these skills, and even fewer have the time or motivation to take on these tasks.

Comprehensive Service Centers. Comprehensive centers provide the full range of activities described above. These centers serve as a focal point for students and faculty interested in volunteer activities. At several institutions, the centers were located in small houses, contributing a strong identity to the center and providing students with a comfortable gathering place. Because co-curricular student placements tend to dominate the work of these centers, we found that six of the eight centers we visited report to Student Affairs and only two to Academic Affairs.

Comprehensive centers are typically managed by staff rather than faculty and often employ students to coordinate programs. In more stable situations, centers are funded as line items in campus budgets or provided with endowments. Less stable organizations rely on grants and other temporary resources.

The existence of a comprehensive center practically guarantees an ongoing program of service on campus. With its physical presence established in a well-known location, a center takes on a life of its own, making it less vulnerable to budget cuts and political maneuvering. At all sites we visited that had comprehensive centers, the directors expressed confidence in the sustainment of their program.

The Bifurcated Model. On five campuses visited, a unit housed within Academic Affairs administered course-based service-learning, and a unit housed within Student Affairs administered co-curricular service activities. The purpose of this bifurcation was to achieve credibility for course-based service-learning among faculty. For example, one respondent explained that faculty "have a jaundiced view of many of the things happening that are not 'academic.'" For this reason, several sites were reluctant to link course-based service to existing volunteer activities operating under the auspices of Student Affairs.

In most but not all cases, faculty direct the academic centers while staff direct the co-curricular centers. In some cases, the academic service-learning centers are formal entities with permanent staff and budgets. In other cases, the academic centers operate informally, as a special project of a faculty member.

Bifurcated centers may be necessary to earn legitimacy for course-based service-learning and promote faculty involvement and leadership. Comprehensive centers, on the other hand, offer the benefits of simplicity, since all service-related activities are coordinated by a single organization.

Faculty Involvement

Reflecting the LSAHE emphasis on integrating service into course work, 16 of the 18 single institution grantees visited had incorporated one or more for-credit courses into their LSAHE-related activities. Nonetheless, researchers came away from the majority of site visits convinced that service-learning occupies a marginal and somewhat tenuous status within higher education institutions.

The marginalization of service-learning is reflected in the small number of courses offered at most institutions. About half of the institutions we visited, including three large comprehensive universities, offered fewer than ten service-learning courses. The highest proportion of faculty involved in service-learning was 20 percent.

The low rates of faculty participation are easily understood as the product of institutional incentive systems. Faculty repeatedly told researchers that participation in service-learning was irrelevant to promotion and tenure decisions and that they lacked the extra time required to develop and teach service-learning courses. Some junior faculty were advised that participation in service-learning would hinder their chances of achieving tenure. Other faculty resist participation on philosophical grounds, because they believe that service-learning is less rigorous relative to other pedagogical approaches. This perception can be reinforced by organizational factors. For example, almost half the programs responding to the Accomplishments Survey are housed outside of the Academic Affairs division of their institution.

Program directors had limited success in attracting faculty to service-learning beyond a small core of supporters. Typically, programs began with a small group of faculty participants whose enthusiasm influenced a second group of faculty to become involved. Beyond this point, the addition of new courses progressed very slowly. Many administrators would agree with a respondent who said, "There is no widespread faculty interest in service-learning, but there is a core of faculty committed to it."

Faculty disinterest in or resistance to service-learning has several negative effects. First, it increases the difficulty of integrating service into core courses as opposed to electives. Of the 18 institutions we visited, only two had service-learning course requirements for several programs; the others offered service-learning courses only or predominantly on an elective basis, with the result that relatively few students gained exposure to service-learning. Second, a low rate of faculty participation reduces the sustainability of service-learning courses due to high turnover among nontenured instructors. Third, reliance on nontenured instructors may reduce the quality of the courses, particularly with regard to reflection. (Although some would argue that nontenured personnel may be excellent instructors, the tenured faculty presumably have the deepest understanding of their disciplines and hence are in the best position to help students link their experiences as service providers to disciplinary content.)

Finally, the limited participation of tenured faculty creates a "cycle of marginalization" that in the long run increases the difficulty of curricular integration. That is, the over-representation of nontenured instructors in service-learning may contribute to the perception among tenured faculty that service-learning is an inappropriate activity for them to undertake. Thus, the expectation that the number or proportion of tenured faculty involved in service-learning will increase over time may not be fulfilled if service-learning becomes identified with ancillary, and lower status, members of the college community.

By contrast, the few programs that had strong faculty support were much better able to integrate service into the curriculum, offering the highest number of service-learning courses. LSAHE-supported programs used a variety of strategies to boost faculty participation in service-learning. Financial support, such as stipends, release time, and mini-grants, enabled faculty to spend time on development, attend off-site conferences and workshops, and purchase materials. Workshops, seminars, and brown bag lunches offered faculty an opportunity to learn more about service-learning, how to modify and improve their courses, and how to structure reflection exercises. In addition, many programs provided staff support, so faculty could delegate the time-consuming and difficult work of identifying service sites and placing and monitoring students.

A small number of faculty were able to leverage the time-consuming development of a service-learning course by linking the service experience to their research and generating publications and professional presentations. In this way, service-learning helped faculty advance their careers, contradicting the complaint that participation in service-learning hinders faculty prospects for tenure or promotion.

Leadership Support

Research in organizational development has repeatedly demonstrated the crucial role of organizational leaders in creating change. The concept of a single committed individual as the driving force or "change agent" behind a program's success extends back at least 20 years (Berman and McLaughlin, 1978). It is not surprising that the site visits underscore the importance of administrative and faculty leadership support in helping institutions achieve their service-learning objectives.

Charismatic Leaders. At many of the sites visited, charismatic leaders were effective champions of service-learning. By "charismatic leaders," we mean people who can marshal resources and convince others to participate on the basis of their influence and informal relationships, not necessarily their formal positions. To a great extent, however, "charisma" is in the eye of the beholder, and hence we do not attempt to quantify this dimension. Some examples may suffice instead:

- The campus minister in one liberal arts college was a powerful spokesperson for service-learning, effectively lobbying faculty and administrators (including the president) to support service-learning courses, even though he had no formal authority over curriculum.
- A faculty member in a research university was so enthusiastic about his service-learning program that he obtained both institutional funding and a variety of external grants despite many competing needs and demands.
- Through sheer force of personality and enthusiasm, a faculty member in a community college was able to persuade at least a half dozen colleagues to teach service-learning courses.

Charismatic leaders can greatly facilitate efforts to involve faculty and secure administrative commitments of funds, space, or staff for service programs. When a faculty or staff member is the charismatic leader, she or he may work well beyond any compensated time to recruit community agencies, attract faculty, and encourage students to participate. The leader's vision and enthusiasm may also lend a sense of importance, direction, and energy to service programs. The downside to this form of leadership is that eventually these people leave either the program or the institution or turn their attention to other priorities or opportunities. So long as the commitments and relationships are personality based, rather than institutionally formalized, the program will be vulnerable to changes in leadership.

Institutions without charismatic leaders depend on administrative support and student enthusiasm to maintain their service-learning courses and programs. The major difficulty facing the institution under these conditions is recruiting faculty, since as discussed above, there is considerable faculty resistance to service-learning.

Administrative Leaders. In a number of institutions we visited, the primary impetus for service-learning came from high-level administrators, such as the president, provost, or chief student affairs officer. Such administrative leaders can often marshal resources and interest faculty because of both the personal relationships they have cultivated and their authority and status. The site visits provided numerous examples of the benefits of strong administrative leadership:

- A provost at a large comprehensive university was instrumental in obtaining an LSAHE grant for his institution and asked several junior faculty to get involved. They reported that as newcomers to the campus, they felt obligated to agree, but later became thankful for the opportunity. All of these faculty have continued to offer service-learning courses even though the provost has left the institution.
- At another large comprehensive university, the president allocated a large brick house for a center site, along with sufficient money for renovations and start-up.
- A community college president ensured that the institution paid the full costs of release time for senior faculty to serve in a leadership position within a new service center.

However, some of the programs we observed were overly dependent upon these leaders. For example, one grantee explained that a dean had provided the program with discretionary funds of $15,000 per year. Unfortunately, when the dean left, his successor did not support service-learning to the same degree, and program staff were concerned that they would lose these funds. Similarly, another grantee related that their project was the "pet" of the provost. When a new provost was appointed, the program was left with no budget allocation for the following year, and the program is still struggling to recover. In these institutions, support for service-learning was linked to a single administrator and was not broadly accepted as an institutional priority.

On the other hand, programs lacking administrative leadership struggled to survive. External fund-raising became a necessity, but the programs were often a low priority for campus development officers and were sometimes barred from approaching foundations or funders for which the institution had other requests. These programs were often relegated to tiny offices in inconvenient locations, lacked adequate computer equipment or office support, and were excluded from institutional planning and decisionmaking processes. For example, some service-learning program directors were not involved in campus efforts to reform undergraduate education, and others were not involved in strategic, academic, or even curricular planning. This situation does not necessarily reflect active hostility among administrative leaders, but rather the simple lack of a high-level advocate.

Programmatic Leaders. In almost every site visited, the LSAHE program directors provided day-to-day leadership of service-learning programs. These leaders were a diverse group, ranging from tenured faculty to temporary staff. Some were long-time institutional employees; others were new employees hired to run the LSAHE grant. Generally, the program directors we visited were knowledgeable about and committed to service-learning. The vast majority worked far more than the hours for which they were paid, reflecting both their personal dedication and the heavy workload their jobs entailed (particularly in relation to available resources).

The site visits suggest that relatively few program directors are attending to the development of future program leaders, in part because there has been only a moderate amount of turnover at the project director level. Turnover at this level has had mixed effects on the programs.

In summary, strong support from institutional leaders is critical to the development and sustainment of service-learning programs. In all sites visited that had successful implementation, administrators or senior faculty members were visible and vocal supporters of service-learning. Reliance on a single change agent, however, is a risky proposition. Service-learning programs must cultivate the next generation of leaders and ensure that their programs become part of the routine operations of their institutions. In this way, "institutional memory" and expertise will continue even after the leader is gone.

A Service Tradition

Overriding almost all barriers in the promotion of service programs is an institution's explicit or implicit tradition of service. The site visits suggest that several types of institutions provide especially fertile ground for the development of service-learning programs. First, many historically black colleges and universities have a strong tradition of service, and some have incorporated service to community into their missions. Second, church-affiliated institutions appear more likely than secular institutions to place a high value on service. Third, campuses with a strong social action imperative may view service as a natural channel for ameliorating social problems. Finally, we observed a number of very young institutions investing in service-learning. With the exception of this last group, these institutions have usually emphasized co-curricular rather than course-based service. Nonetheless, the institutions may have both the infrastructure and the value system needed for curricular integration of service.

Although service-learning practitioners and proponents can take a variety of concrete steps to establish service centers, involve faculty, and develop leadership, there is little that can be done to affect an institution's traditions and history. Perhaps the broader lesson emerging from the site visits is that institutions are most likely to develop strong service-learning programs when they can link service to institutional values, traditions, and missions.

SUMMARY OF CONCLUSIONS

The grantees included in RAND's evaluation made substantial progress in three of four institutional outcome areas. They expanded service opportunities for students, integrated service into courses, and forged strong community relations. The results for the fourth area—building sustainable programs—are not yet available, but the evidence so far suggests that as many as half of all programs may face difficulties in maintaining their progress.

Service programs face many barriers. Foremost among these is faculty resistance due to the extra burden that service-learning courses impose and, in many cases, skepticism about the value and effectiveness of service-learning. Administrative disinterest can also be problematic, especially when service-learning programs are hindered in fund-raising and efforts to coordinate their activities with other campus initiatives.

Four factors are particularly effective in promoting strong service programs. First, service centers play a crucial role in coordinating and institutionalizing service activities. Faculty involvement is also critical, but site visits indicated that faculty involvement is often limited to a small core of enthusiasts. Third, leadership support plays an important role in establishing, enhancing, and sustaining service programs. The sites we visited relied on both charismatic and administrative leaders but were in some cases overly dependent upon personal, rather than institutional, support. Finally, a strong institutional tradition of service is helpful in developing service-learning programs.

7. WHAT WAS THE RETURN ON INVESTMENT TO COMMUNITIES?

INTRODUCTION

A major purpose of the federal investment in LSAHE is to help higher education institutions overcome the start-up costs of service-learning programs. Grants are limited to three years, and institutions are prompted to pursue sustainable programs, although it is possible for grantees to reapply with a new program proposal after their initial grant ends. An important future return on the federal investment will arise from the colleges and universities that continue service-learning programs after federal funding ends. We consider the investments made in LSAHE-funded programs and the resulting services produced for communities.

This chapter places a valuation on the services produced by LSAHE-funded programs in comparison to the resources they consume. The computation of resources depends on allocating federal and local resources to programs that perform direct service. The valuation of services uses a comparison to part-time temporary workers that might be hired by community agencies to produce equivalent service. While the measures of valuation and resources are not perfect, they are strong indicators of the efficiency of LSAHE-funded programs in producing community service.

Producing community service is only one objective of LSAHE. As other chapters detail, there is moderate evidence for benefits to students from service-learning, especially when certain structuring elements are in place. In addition, we know that LSAHE-funded institutions developed a significant number of courses incorporating service over the period of the grants. This analysis of return on investment does not attempt to directly value the benefits to students or institutions, although some of the institutional benefits are evident in the pattern of increasing service over time.

This analysis, however, can only consider the three-year period of grant funding, not later activity. Because of the relatively steep start-up costs involved in these programs, this three-year window is a serious limitation. It is crucial to know whether the institutions and communities can sustain these programs after federal grants end.

DIFFICULTIES IN COMPUTING RESOURCES

To compute the return on investment, we estimate the value of services and compare it to the resources invested. The computation of resources and value is complicated by several factors. In this section, we explain the difficulties in computing resources and how we overcome those difficulties. The next section treats the computation of value.

A major difficulty is that programs combine funding from several funding sources in a way that makes it impossible to attribute a specific effect to each source of funding. Figure 7.1 illustrates the relationship among the major resources, expenses, and activities in LSAHE-funded programs. The institutions allocate internally and externally supplied resources to support various expenditures and activities. Externally supplied resources include LSAHE grants and subgrants, as well as other sponsored funding for service-learning. Internally supplied resources are those provided by the program's host institution. These internally supplied resources are divided into two categories: cash and in-kind. Cash resources include salaries, fringe benefits, and other direct costs of operations. In-kind resources include the program's share of common expenses, such as facilities maintenance, utilities, institutional management, and general overhead. As Figure 7.1 indicates, it is not generally possible to connect a specific source of funds with specific activities.

This analysis relies primarily on data from the Annual Accomplishments Surveys. The Accomplishments Survey includes detailed questions on the service performed by volunteers in each program. The Fiscal 1996 and 1997 Accomplishments Surveys also include detailed questions on resources, including grant funds, matching funds, and the percentage of matching funds that are in-kind. Although these questions were not included in the Fiscal 1995 survey, CNS has resource data for direct grantees showing grant and matching funds for these programs.

To some extent, in-kind resources may represent costs that the institution would incur with or without the LSAHE-funded program. But if the space for LSAHE-funded programs could be used for other functions, then space costs represent a true resource contribution to the LSAHE-funded program, since they are an opportunity cost for the institution. It can be debated whether all of the programs' reported match in resources should be counted, because some of the in-kind contributions may not represent true costs or opportunity costs to the institutions. The survey data indicate that slightly more of the matching funds come from in-kind contributions as opposed to cash. For Fiscal 1996, which we believe to be typical, we

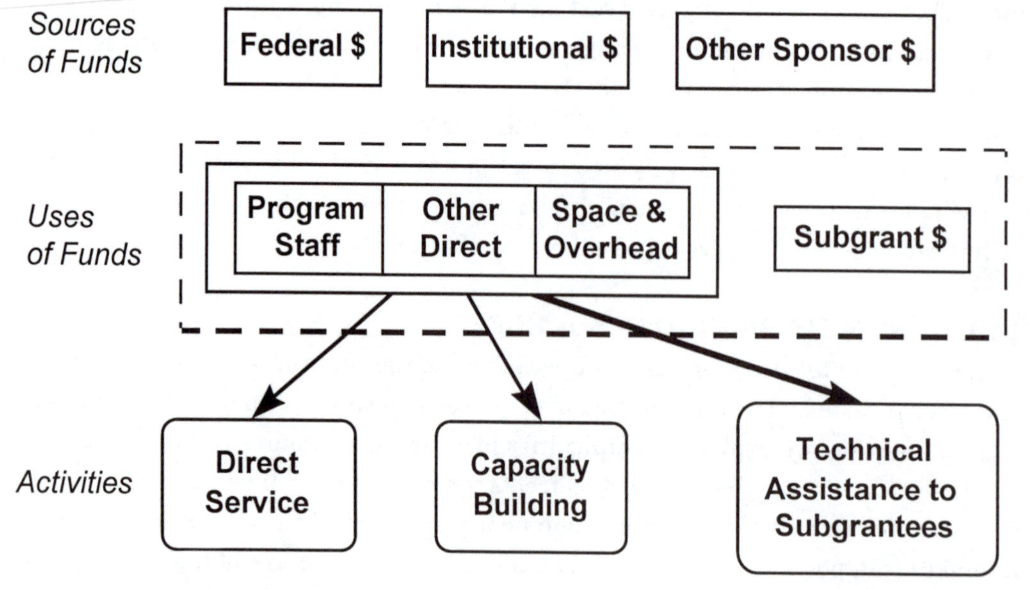

Figure 7.1—Flow of Resources and Resulting Activities in LSAHE Programs

found that in-kind contributions represented about 54 percent of the cash total (grant plus cash match). This rate is high if it represents indirect costs for facilities and administration. However, it may include costs, such as faculty time, that did not represent budget items to the survey respondents even though they are standard direct costs to colleges. Because we were not able to make a more refined categorization of these resources, all reported matching funds were treated as true resources in the analysis.

LSAHE-funded programs perform three basic types of activities: (1) direct service, (2) capacity building, and (3) administration. Direct service activities support the generation of current service to recipients. These activities include liaison between service-learning faculty and community agencies. The goal of capacity building activities is to develop future infrastructure for service rather than produce service immediately. Examples of capacity building are developing a community service center and devising new curricula incorporating service-learning.

Consortium programs do not engage in direct service. These programs distribute much of their grant funds to subgrantees. But consortia also expend resources in support of consortium functions, such as selecting subgrantee programs, allocating funding, reporting, and providing technical assistance. Direct grant consortia receive funding directly from CNS. Subgrant consortia receive funding from a direct grantee and then further distribute funds to subsubgrantees. In addition to the consortia, which perform no direct service, there are single institution direct grant and subgrant programs that perform direct service *and* make subgrants. A program like this is a hybrid between a pure direct service program and a consortium.

Since LSAHE-funded programs combine funding from many sources, we estimated the total resources expended by each program during each year. This includes LSAHE grant or subgrant funding, as well as matching funds provided by campuses or other parties. We did not include any estimate of CNS overhead in administering the LSAHE grant program.

We allocated resources to the programs that were intended to perform direct service. Thus, resources of each consortium were distributed to the consortium's subgrantees (in proportion to the amount of each subgrant). For programs that combined direct service with subgranting, we allocated a portion of resources in proportion to the amount of each subgrant. Because of this method of allocating resources to subgrantees, consortium programs themselves do not have a computed return on investment in this analysis. Rather, a consortium's programmatic and financial structure affects the return on investment of each of its subgrantees. So although consortia affect the return on investment, consortium programs do not appear as program observations in the analyses reported here.

Resources consumed by consortia were substantial. In most cases, the consortia expended more themselves than they issued in subgrants. For direct grant consortia, the median value for consortium spending was $1.60 per dollar in subgrants. For subgrant consortia, the median value for consortium spending (including the direct grant and the subgrant levels) was $3.80 per dollar in subsubgrants. While these values seem very high, the consortium structure may be efficient. The consortium allows many programs to share costs of capacity building, such as writing manuals, holding symposia, and developing curricula. Our analysis helps to indicate whether these high consortium costs are offset by value produced by the programs within consortia.

DIFFICULTIES IN COMPUTING VALUE OF SERVICE

The determination of return on investment requires aligning expenditures with benefits. However, the "base" on which grantees report benefits and the "base" on which they report resources are not necessarily the same. The Fiscal 1996 and 1997 Accomplishments Surveys attempt to mitigate this problem by asking respondents to report all service from programs that receive LSAHE funding, even though only part of the funding comes from LSAHE. The analysis depends on being able to compare the resources and benefits as reported on the survey. Because this alignment was not part of the Fiscal 1995 Accomplishments Survey, those data may be less accurate.

There are significant challenges in computing the value of service. The ideal method of valuing the service performed by students participating in LSAHE-funded programs would be to compute the impact on their communities. However, considering the large number of activities and the small amount of time contributed by each volunteer, it would be prohibitively costly to evaluate the direct impact of each volunteer's effort. Instead, our approach to valuing the service of student volunteers is to estimate the costs that community agencies would incur to hire hourly workers to perform the same functions as the students. Because students typically work a few hours per week, this comparison to part-time hourly workers is appropriate.

This approach is equivalent to asking the question, Is it better to purchase services directly for communities or to give resources to colleges and universities to build service-learning programs that produce community service? The LSAHE programs give resources to colleges and universities and, in effect, ask them to develop a variety of local service activities. We can measure the extent of those activities, and we know the level of LSAHE funding going to college or university programs. But what of the value of the services provided? Our method imputes a cost of providing these services. Thus, taking the variety and scale of services as given, we ask what this bundle would have cost if the services had been purchased directly. Once the valuation of services is obtained, we can compare it to the LSAHE funding level. If the valuation of services exceeds the LSAHE funding level, then the LSAHE programs have succeeded in providing the bundle of services at lower cost than if the services had been purchased directly. In other words, the LSAHE has created what we will call a positive return on investment. This approach does not directly consider whether the services that LSAHE-funded programs provide are valued in the community. If community agencies were provided funding to procure services, they might choose services other than the ones performed by these programs. In such cases, the value we estimate here might be overstated.

To evaluate the quality of LSAHE volunteers' service, our Fiscal 1995 and 1996 Community Impact Surveys asked community partners to compare "paid service or equivalent skill level providers." As reported in Table 5.5, the average of the respondent ratings of the effectiveness of LSAHE volunteer services was 3.2 and 3.0 (over the two years surveyed) on a five-point scale (where 1 = much worse, 3 = about the same, 5 = much better). These results indicate that the community partners felt that, on the average, the LSAHE volunteers performed at about the level of paid service providers. If these survey responses accurately reflect the value of the participants' service, then market-equivalent wage rates will accurately reflect what community organizations would have to pay in the market for the same services

The same community surveys yield an indication of whether LSAHE-funded programs are meeting community demands. Table 5.4 shows that over 90 percent of community organizations believed that the benefits of working with LSAHE-funded programs outweighed the costs from their perspective. About 75 percent felt that the "benefits far outweighed the costs."

The community organizations' ratings of volunteers' effectiveness in individual areas indicate that, in every area, the student volunteers were effective. Overall, the biggest suggestion for improvement was that LSAHE-funded programs increase the number of students participating. If students were performing service in areas that communities did not value, we would not expect the communities to rate students as effective and to seek more student volunteers. While these opinions do not conclusively demonstrate that community organizations would purchase these same services, they do suggest a high valuation in the community. One specific piece of evidence for the community value of the service comes from the site visits. During the second-year site visits, the interview team asked the community organizations what they would be willing to pay the volunteers. In almost all cases, the community organizations' valuations were higher than the one produced by the method we used. Consequently, we believe that unadjusted market-equivalent wage rates provide a reasonably appropriate way to value the student volunteers' contribution to communities.

The procedure we used to compute the value of service can be summarized as follows. First, to estimate the cost of hiring hourly workers, we defined job titles equivalent to each task and researched average wages for those jobs. The source for wage data is America's Job Bank. This bank combines employment positions listed in state-level data systems in the 50 United States. While state participation varies, the positions represent a range of states. To eliminate variation in the results from wage changes (which were minor over this period), we used a single average wage for all three years' calculations.

In keeping with standard economic practices, we added a 20 percent allowance to the base wage for *legally required* employer-paid fringe benefits (Worker's Compensation, Social Security Tax, Medicare Tax, State and Federal Unemployment Tax, State Disability Insurance). We added a further 20 percent on the base wage plus fringe amount to represent the premium that a temporary service firm would charge to fill these positions. While 20 percent is lower than many firms would actually charge, we believe that it fairly represents the costs of recruiting and matching employees to jobs. In the LSAHE-funded programs, the campus program performs these functions, so we included this factor in the value of service provided.

The value of service per hour averaged over all specifically defined tasks is about $13.00 in each year. Activities that were classified as other than a defined task area were assigned this average value.

The calculations of return on investment in this chapter do not include returns experienced by student participants in LSAHE-funded programs or by colleges and universities as institutions. Such returns, if any, would increase the total return on investment over the levels reported here. Instead, we focus just on the returns to the communities or community agencies that received the services provided through the LSAHE-funded programs.

VALUE INCREASES SHARPLY OVER THREE YEARS

We found strong evidence that programs are on track to overcome their start-up costs. The estimated value of services increased over the three years we studied, while resources remained level or decreased. Although the programs did not repay their entire investment over the three-year time horizon, they will more than repay the investment if they can sustain these returns past the third year. In a later section of this chapter, we show that there is some reason to believe that programs will sustain themselves, although the evidence available at this time is necessarily weak.

Given our goal of examining how resources and value compare over time, our analyses focused mainly on the grantees we could track over the three-year period. The structure of the LSAHE program means that direct grantees whose grants are renewed from year to year represent the same programs over time. But the same does not hold for subgrantees or subsubgrantees. Although a given higher education institution may receive a subgrant in two or three years, it is not possible for us to tell whether the program funded is the same over time. Consequently, we restricted the main analyses to direct grantees with complete data for all three grant years. There were 27 such programs. All of these 27 programs performed some direct service in each of the three years (but we would have included a program even if it had performed no direct service in one or more years).[1]

We will examine the data in several ways to support the point that value increases sharply compared to resources over the three years. First, we examine the total reported resources and value for the 27 direct grant programs described above. Then we look at the median values in this group to verify that the pattern is not unduly influenced by a few programs. Our third exploration uses statistical tests to confirm that these increases are most likely not accidental, but represent significant effects. Our fourth analysis consists of comparing the results for the 27 direct grantees to all available data for Fiscal 1996 and 1997.

The first examination is of the total reported resources and value. The increase in value, shown in Figure 7.2, is striking. In Fiscal 1995, the programs produced very little

---

[1]One direct grant program did not fit the LSAHE model described here in that it was entirely devoted to producing training and materials to be used in K-12 service learning. We treated this program as a consortium, but one whose subgrantees were outside the scope of our analysis. Therefore, this program's resources and value are omitted from the calculations here.

value compared to their resources. In Fiscal 1996, value almost equals resources. In Fiscal 1997, value modestly exceeds resources. Over the three-year study period, the total value of $18 million amounts to about 60 percent of the total resources invested, $31 million. These numbers are subject to a great deal of uncertainty, especially in the valuing of the benefits. Therefore, interpretation of small differences is inappropriate.

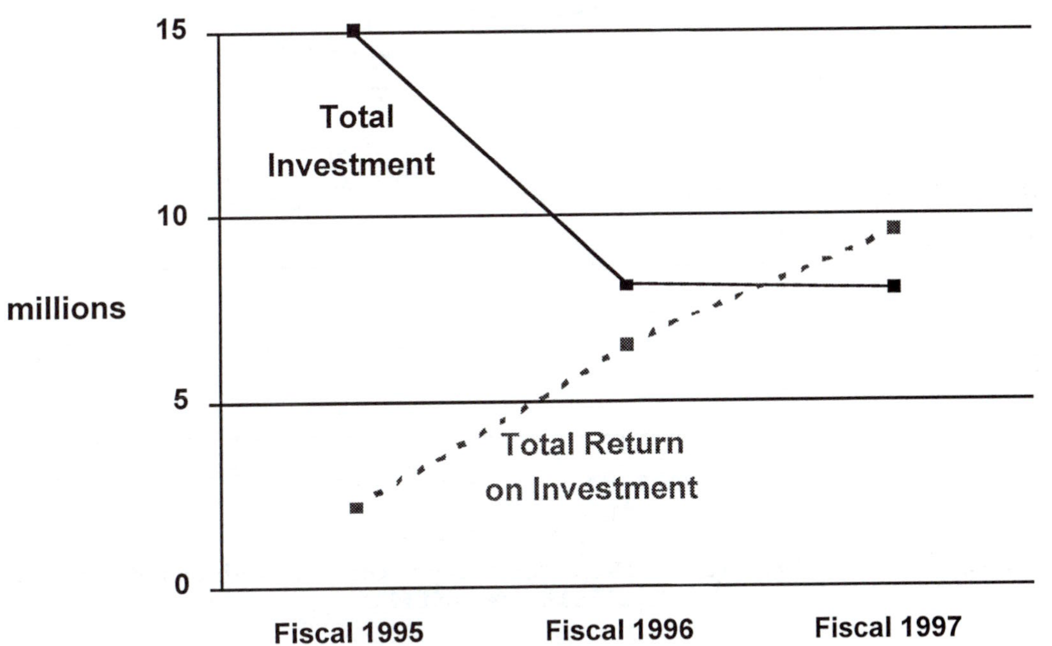

Figure 7.2—Total Resources and Value for the 27 Direct Grantees with Complete Data for Fiscal 1995, 1996, and 1997

Which component of value is responsible for the increase in value over the three years? There are two components of value: the number of hours of service and the average value per hour. For LSAHE, the increase in value is due to increasing hours of service provided, not to higher average value per hour. In fact, the average value per hour is somewhat higher in Fiscal 1995 than in the later years. Figure 7.2 shows that value increases from 1995 to 1996 to 1997. Although the average value per hour is declining somewhat over time, the hours of service are increasing even more, resulting in an overall increase in value.

Our second investigation of the return on investment for this group uses the medians of the same 27 programs to verify that the pattern of Figure 7.2 is not influenced unduly by a few programs with very large value of service or very large resources. The median values are not subject to much influence by these outliers and so are a more robust measure of return on investment. The medians of this group of programs (which are shown in Figure 7.3) are consistent with the results in Figure 7.2, although the Fiscal 1995 investment is more level with 1996 and 1997, unlike in Figure 7.2. Although the value does not rise above resources in Fiscal 1997, it certainly increases over the three years. Taking the sum of these medians, about half of the three-year investment is returned in value. This is consistent with the findings above, where about 60 percent of total investment was returned in value to communities.[2]

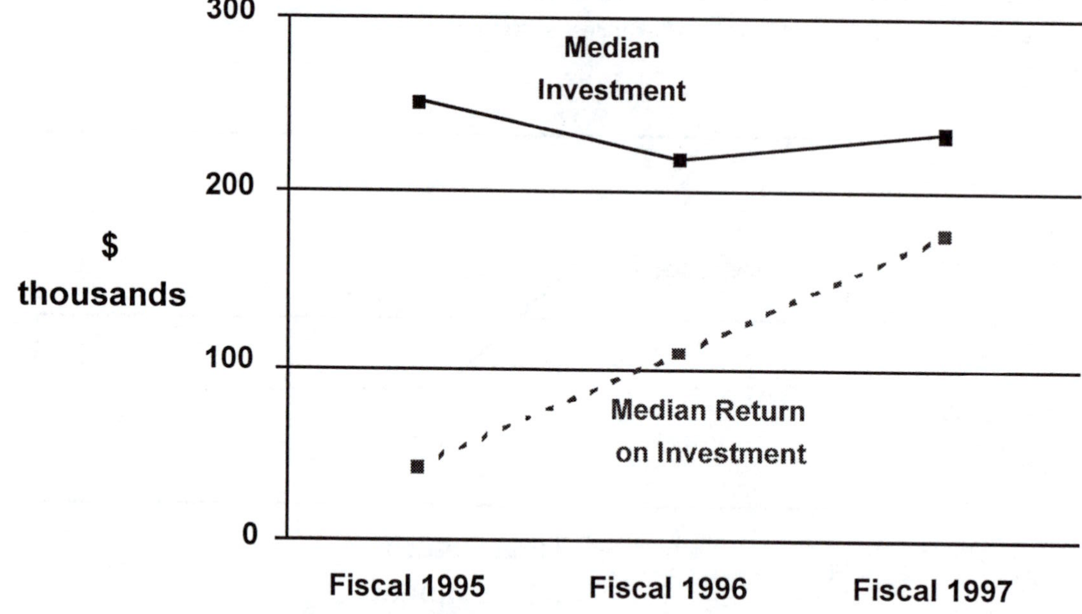

Figure 7.3—Median Resources and Value for 27 Direct Grantees with Complete Data for Fiscal 1995, 1996, and 1997

Our third investigation of return on investment for these 27 programs uses statistical tests to confirm the validity of the results graphed in Figures 7.2 and 7.3. We conducted statistical tests on the ratio of value to resources in each year and found that the increases in the figures are highly statistically significant.

To conduct these tests, we use the ratio of value to resources in each year for each program, called the return on investment (ROI) ratio. The plain ROI ratio is necessarily skewed heavily to the right, since it is bounded below by zero but has unlimited upper bound (and a center of mass near one).[3] The log of the ROI ratio yields a statistic that is much more symmetrically distributed. In addition, the log ROI ratio reduces the influence of large positive outliers, which are present in our data as a result of a few programs that had very large values in comparison to their resources.

Tables 7.1 and 7.2 summarize these calculations. Using a paired t-test between Fiscal 1995 and Fiscal 1996 yields a statistically significant increase (at the 0.01 level). The increase between Fiscal 1996 and Fiscal 1997 is also quite significant (at the 0.02 level).

---

[2]The medians of both resources and value are substantially lower than the means because of the strong skewness in the distributions (see next footnote).

[3]The skewness of the Fiscal 1997 ROI ratio is 3.5, indicating strong skewness to the right (positive direction). In contrast, the skewness of the log ROI ratio is -0.3, almost perfectly symmetrical.

These results confirm that the pattern in Figures 7.2 and 7.3 is a valid one: the increase in value over time is very, very unlikely to be from chance.

Table 7.1

ROI Ratios for 27 Direct Grant Programs

	Grant Year		
	Fiscal 1995	Fiscal 1996	Fiscal 1997
Mean of ROI ratio	0.31	0.63	1.19
Mean of log ROI ratio	-1.93	-0.77	-0.27
Variance of log ROI ratio	2.41	1.01	1.40

Table 7.2

Comparison of ROI Ratios Between Years

	Comparison of Fiscal 1995 and 1996	Comparison of Fiscal 1996 and 1997
Paired t-test value	3.82	2.43
Significance (p value)	0.0007	0.0221

The fourth analysis compares the results for the 27 direct grantees to a broader set of programs and finds that the pattern in Figures 7.2 and 7.3 is supported by the experience of the broader set of programs. Specifically, we have complete data on value and resources for 219 Fiscal 1996 programs and 160 Fiscal 1997 programs. Because the Fiscal 1995 resource data are available only for direct grantees, we do not have results for Fiscal 1995 on all programs. Again, consortia are not included as observations, but their data are used in computing return on investment for all subgrants and subsubgrants.

Table 7.3 reports the Fiscal 1996 ROI ratio by program type. The ROI ratio is calculated as the ratio of the value of service to the resources expended for each program *during that year*. For all 219 programs, the ROI ratio was 0.7, compared to 0.8 for the 27 programs that were tracked over three years. Although these values are very close, there may be a modest difference between the ROI ratios because new programs were starting up during Fiscal 1996. If the pattern in Figure 7.2 holds for most programs, the new start-up programs would experience very low ROI ratios while the more established programs experienced higher ROI ratios. On average, this yields the ROI ratio seen in Table 7.3.

Table 7.4 reports the same data for the Fiscal 1997 programs. Recall that except for the direct grantees that we track from year to year, the rest of the programs reported in Tables 7.3 and 7.4 may undergo substantial turnover and redefinition. Hence, it may not be appropriate to compare the ROI ratios across the two years. Nevertheless, we did note that the Fiscal 1997 ROI ratios for the 27 direct grantees we tracked over three years (1.2) were very similar to the 1.3 value in Table 7.4. This may mean that the start-up effects are diminishing by Fiscal 1997. Even though some of the subgrants and subsubgrants are less established, the large amount of capacity building by the consortia in Fiscal 1995 and 1996 may be helping them to get a faster start than their subgrant counterparts had in Fiscal 1996.

Table 7.3

Fiscal 1996 ROI Ratio

	N	Average ROI Ratio	Sum of Value ($ millions)	Sum of Resources ($ millions)
All programs combined	219	0.7	16.0	23.4
Direct grants	70	0.7	11.4	16.6
Subgrants	125	0.8	4.4	5.7
Subsubgrants	24	0.2	0.2	1.1

NOTE: Consortium-level programs are not included. Consortium-funded programs are included as subgrants and subsubgrants.

Table 7.4

Fiscal 1997 ROI Ratio

	N	Average ROI Ratio	Sum of Value ($ millions)	Sum of Resources ($ millions)
All programs combined	160	1.3	22.3	17.5
Direct grants	50	1.4	17.3	12.5
Subgrants	86	1.0	4.3	4.5
Subsubgrants	24	1.4	0.7	0.5

NOTE: Consortium-level programs are not included. Consortium-funded programs are included as subgrants and subsubgrants.

The data in Tables 7.3 and 7.4 are consistent with the findings for the 27 direct grantees, i.e., the ROI ratio increases over time. Some of this increase may stem from policy changes at CNS and/or the consortia, including the buildup of capacity at consortia. The increase also may be due to the capacity built at individual program sites. The similarity of the ROI ratios for subgrantees to the grantees indicates that the large start-up costs incurred by some direct grantees in Fiscal 1995 (as shown in Figure 7.2) may not be incurred by future grantees, since they can benefit from the growing infrastructure in service-learning developed through LSAHE-funded programs.

Overall, all four analyses of return on investment support the identical conclusion: value increased sharply compared to resources invested over the three years of the LSAHE grant. It does not appear that the programs fully repay their total investment within three years, but if they can sustain this pattern of accomplishment into the future, they will amply repay the initial investment. The next section examines the role of consortia and subgranting in return on investment. The ensuing section then introduces some limited evidence that programs will sustain themselves beyond the end of their grants.

CONSORTIA SEEM ABLE TO OVERCOME HIGH OVERHEAD

In addition to their value in corroborating the increasing return over time, the data in Tables 7.3 and 7.4 can serve as an aid in understanding the effectiveness of consortia and subgranting practices. We find that consortia that operate at a single level (with a direct grant divided into subgrants) appear to be an efficient model for LSAHE. Consortia that operate at a second level (with a direct grant funding subgrant consortia that subdivide money into subsubgrants) may be much less effective, although the results are not conclusive.

We used summary statistics and regression analysis to investigate the role of grant type (direct grant, subgrant, and subsubgrant) and area of service performed (education, health and human needs, public safety, and the environment). We did not find conclusive differences over the years studied.

The ROI ratio for subgrants is generally close to that for direct grants. Since subgrant resources include a share of consortium expenses for administration and technical assistance, if these consortium expenditures are effective, we should see subgrant ROI ratios close to (or even higher than) the direct grant ROI ratios. Over the two years (Fiscal 1996 and 1997), the subgrant and direct grant ROI ratios are similar, suggesting that the high overhead of consortia is offset by commensurate value produced. Two possible benefits from the consortium system are that consortia may promote greater efficiency in how subgrantees spend money and that there may be a direct benefit of the technical assistance function, which can be spread over several subgrantees. It appears the costs of operating consortia are offset by the benefits they generate.

This conclusion is not as clear in the case of subgrant consortia and other subgrant programs that make subsubgrants. Although the Fiscal 1997 ROI ratio is comparable to that for other programs, the Fiscal 1996 ROI ratio is very low. The small number of programs with complete data—24 in each year—indicates the need for caution in interpreting these results. It may be that the subsubgrants take longer to build their programs because of the deeper organizational structure (spanning three levels instead of two).

But there is some evidence in the Fiscal 1996 data that making subsubgrants may be inefficient because the benefits of efficiency and technical assistance cannot be offset by the overhead of two layers of subgranting (from the direct grantee to the subgrantee and then from the subgrantee to the subsubgrantee).

Overall, the benefits of one level of consortia are well established by these results. The effort by consortia to select subgrantees and provide technical assistance and infrastructure appears to pay off. In the case of two-level consortia, the evidence is mixed. Further years of data collection would help to establish whether the two-level consortia exhibit sustained value commensurate with the resources that their structure consumes.

PROGRAMS ARE MOVING TOWARD SUSTAINING THEMSELVES

Only time will tell if programs continue beyond the grant's end. We do have some limited evidence that programs are moving toward sustaining themselves. Between Fiscal 1996 and Fiscal 1997, the average program in the group of 27 direct grantees received less in grant funds and supplied more in matching funds, for an overall increase in funding. As a percentage of total Fiscal 1996 resources, these programs, on average, experienced a decrease of 15 percent in grant funds. They increased matching funds, on average, 8 percent. Because the matching funds are larger than grant funds, the increase in matching funds offsets the decrease in grant funds, resulting in an overall increase in resources of 1 percent from Fiscal 1996 to Fiscal 1997 (unadjusted for inflation). In other words, there is almost no change in overall resources, but there is an important shift away from grants and toward matching funds.

Among these 27 programs, 23 received smaller CNS grants in Fiscal 1997 compared to Fiscal 1996. Of these 23 programs, 15 increased matching funds and eight decreased matching funds. This suggests that many programs are maintaining a stable level of resources despite reductions in CNS grants.

Because of the small number of programs and high variation around these averages, we are again concerned about the reliability of these values. To establish the significance of these results, we used regression analysis to relate the change in matching funds to the change in grant funds between Fiscal 1996 and Fiscal 1997.[4] The regressions (shown in Table 7.5) are not conclusive, but they do suggest that programs experiencing a decrease in CNS grants increase their matching funds. The coefficient estimate of 1.19 means that for every dollar the grant decreases, the matching funds increase by $1.19. The exact size of this coefficient is uncertain. We cannot state that it is different from 1, for example, although it is different from zero at almost the 10 percent level. While this level of precision is insufficient to make firm conclusions, the regression results combined with the raw statistics support the notion that programs are substituting matching funds for grant funds.

Table 7.5

Regression of Change in Matching Funds/Total Fiscal 1996 Resources

Variable	Estimate	t statistic	p value
Constant	0.07	0.80	0.44
Change in grant funds/total Fiscal 1996 resources	1.19	1.65	0.11
R^2	11%		

N = 23 direct grantees experiencing a reduction in CNS grants.

The information available at this time suggests that programs are moving in the direction of sustaining themselves. It is not possible to extrapolate from the average 15 percent reduction in grant amounts in Fiscal 1997 to a 100 percent reduction in Fiscal 1998

[4]The values used in this regression are normalized by dividing both change in matching funds and change in grant funds by the total Fiscal 1996 resources. Thus, the variables are the changes expressed as a fraction of total resources. In this way, we can compare large and small programs without giving very large or small weight based on size. The dependent variable is expressed so that a positive value indicates a reduction in grant funds; thus, a positive coefficient indicates substitution of matching funds.

or beyond, but the results shown here are encouraging. Although there may have been pre-existing agreements to maintain funding in the face of planned reductions in the grants, we do not believe this is a significant driver of these results. Only three of the 23 programs experiencing grant reductions increased their matching funds by an amount that closely corresponded to the reduction.[5] Had these pre-existing agreements been widespread, we would have expected a closer match between decreases in grants and increases in matching funds. We do find a modest replacement of CNS grant funds by matching funds in Fiscal 1997. But we do not know whether institutions have access to local funding sources that are capable of replacing the entire CNS grant. If this funding is not available, programs will shrink after the CNS grant ends.

SUMMARY OF CONCLUSIONS

Our analysis of the return on investment in LSAHE-funded programs used RAND's survey data to assess both the value of service and the resources consumed by programs that received LSAHE funding. Since it is not possible to identify a specific federal contribution to the program's outcomes, the return-on-investment calculations consider all resources available to the programs. The measures of resources and value both have significant limitations. Our estimates of returns for communities are based on the efficiency of LSAHE-funded programs as service providers. We did not formally consider the local community's valuation of the services provided.

The pattern of increasing return over time is striking. Our analyses of the 27 direct grantees that we are able to track over three years indicated that value increased markedly from Fiscal 1995 to Fiscal 1996 to Fiscal 1997. Based on the three-year period we analyzed, these programs appear to produce a total value of service for communities that is about 60 percent of total program expenditures. Since the trend is strongly in the direction of increasing value over time, there is reason to believe that there will be long-term positive returns to communities.

Whether these programs will continue to generate substantial value after their grants end is an open question. We are encouraged that between Fiscal 1996 and Fiscal 1997, there was modest but significant replacement of CNS grant funds by local matching funds. This suggests that programs are moving toward sustainability and will continue to generate value for communities in the future. Although we would like to know how programs will react when grant funds are 100 percent withdrawn, we do not have such information. We can observe much more limited substitution in the third grant year. A reduction in the average direct grant of 15 percent was compensated by increasing matching funds between the second and the third grant year. This evidence is encouraging, but the pattern may not continue in the future, when 100 percent of grant funds is withdrawn. In part, local commitment might decline with the complete withdrawal of CNS funding. To the extent that

---

[5]For these purposes, we counted programs that increased matching funds to make up the reduction in grant funds within 25 percent up or down.

LSAHE-funded programs may be offering services that are in low demand by communities, that would further undermine their chances for long-term continuation with local resources.

The consortium structure involves a great deal of resource expenditure by consortia, with smaller amounts of resources flowing to subgrantees. Despite high central expenditures, these types of programs yield a return on investment similar to that for direct grantees. The inconsistent evidence and small number of programs for subsubgrants warrant further attention in the future to determine whether two levels of subgranting are efficient.

While the results to date offer encouragement that these programs can efficiently provide service to local communities, there are also cautionary notes. Capacity building has been a consistently large activity over the three years studied here. If programs are to enhance their efficiency as service providers, it is important to shift activities away from capacity building and toward promotion of direct service in the future. To track this possible shift and to see if programs sustain themselves after federal grants end, it is very important to follow up on at least some of these programs beyond the third year of the grant. These longer-term indicators will be particularly important in assessing the ultimate return on the large start-up investment in these programs.

8. CONCLUSIONS AND RECOMMENDATIONS

The evaluation results indicate that students in LSAHE-supported courses and programs made valuable contributions to meeting educational, public safety, human, and environmental needs of communities. Students enrolled in service-learning courses also showed more growth in civic and life skills than students in traditional courses. Furthermore, LSAHE appears to have boosted institutional support and capacity for service, although more time is needed before the crucial question of sustainability can be addressed. Thus, LSAHE made important gains in each of its three goal areas.

The next three sections each discuss one of the three goals. Within each section, we present our conclusions regarding the extent to which LSAHE achieved the goal, and we describe any limitations or barriers to success. We then discuss the implications of our findings for LSAHE policies and practices and present directions for future research. The last section of the chapter offers five recommendations.

ENGAGING STUDENTS TO MEET EDUCATIONAL, PUBLIC SAFETY, HUMAN, AND ENVIRONMENTAL NEEDS OF COMMUNITIES

Conclusions

LSAHE was a catalyst for mobilizing students to provide volunteer service in their communities. In Fiscal 1997, an average program involved over 60 students providing more than 2,500 hours of service to the community. Much of this service was in the area of education, which was the greatest beneficiary of LSAHE-supported service.

Staff from community organizations participating in this evaluation perceived these service hours as useful in meeting community needs and believed that student volunteers from LSAHE-supported institutions helped them reach more people, provide more services, and improve the overall quality of service.

Limitations or Barriers to Success

Program staff spent only about one-third of their time on direct service activities. More time was devoted to capacity building, such as technical assistance, course development, or producing publications. By encouraging staff to devote more time to direct service and less time to capacity building, LSAHE could further increase its contributions to communities.

In part because so much time was devoted to capacity building, the total cost of LSAHE-supported programs exceeded their value to communities. Thus, communities might have been better able to meet their needs by purchasing services directly, rather than enlisting the support of student volunteers. The capacity building activities to which grantees devoted their time, however, are intended to expand and improve direct service. The evaluation provides indirect support for this objective by demonstrating an increasing return on the LSAHE investment over time. Although this could indicate the effects of capacity building, other explanations are also possible, and the link between capacity building and program effectiveness remains unclear.

Additionally, although LSAHE emphasized course-based service-learning, results indicate that co-curricular programs produced more service hours per student than did course-based service-learning. It is possible that LSAHE's preference for course-based service may have inadvertently reduced the potential contributions of student volunteers to communities, in effect trading off benefits to communities for benefits to students. More research is needed to determine the effects of course-based versus co-curricular service in meeting community needs.

Programmatic Implications

If the primary goal of LSAHE is to serve communities, or if CNS wants to boost the level of service that communities are receiving through LSAHE, program directors should be encouraged to spend more time on direct service and less time on capacity building. In addition, CNS might consider providing stronger controls or guidelines with regard to both direct service and capacity building. For example, LSAHE guidelines might specify the target number of hours that programs are expected to provide. CNS might also consider providing incentives for direct service, such as including direct service hours as a criterion used in decisionmaking about continuation funding.

Directions for Future Research

More research is needed to determine the effects of the LSAHE investment in capacity building and, in particular, whether and when capacity building "pays off" in terms of higher quality, larger, or more-sustainable programs. If it does, the value of LSAHE to communities over time is likely to exceed program costs. In addition, research comparing the effects on communities of course-based versus co-curricular service would be useful.

ENHANCING STUDENTS' LEARNING, THEIR SENSE OF SOCIAL RESPONSIBILITY, AND THEIR LIFE SKILLS

Conclusions

Results are mixed with regard to the LSAHE goal of enhancing students' learning and development. RAND's 1997 Student Survey indicated that participation in service-learning courses was positively associated with self-reported development of civic and life skills, although effect sizes are quite small. For example, students in service-learning courses were more likely than students in nonservice courses to report that the course strengthened their current and expected levels of involvement in addressing social problems, their interpersonal skills, and their understanding of diversity. On the other hand, no association emerged between participation in course-based service-learning and academic or professional skill development. Service-learning students did not report stronger gains than comparison students in writing, quantitative reasoning, or analytic thinking. They were also no more likely to report that the course helped them clarify major or career plans.

Several factors were strongly associated with more-positive service-learning outcomes. Most important is connecting the in-class to the community experience. Other factors associated with positive outcomes are discussing service in class and providing training and supervision for students' service experiences. Students who volunteered for more than 20 hours, were over 25 years of age, and volunteered in areas other than education, health and human needs, the environment, or public safety also reported relatively positive effects of participation in service on their development.

In sum, this goal was partially achieved. This finding is important because most LSAHE program directors and CNS staff assigned it high priority. The intent to enhance student learning is the major reason, for example, that LSAHE emphasizes course-based service-learning as opposed to co-curricular service-learning, community service, or volunteerism.

More positive findings emerge from a 1996 survey by Sax, Astin, and Astin (1996). This student survey found positive effects of participation in service on all outcome areas. However, it was not limited to service-learning, but rather studied the effects of any participation in volunteer service during college.

Limitations or Barriers to Success

The evaluation suggests that LSAHE might have been more successful in achieving this goal if course instructors consistently implemented certain practices. Thus, the barriers to success may well lie in the manner in which service-learning courses were designed and implemented, not with inherent limitations to service-learning.

Programmatic Implications

The survey findings underscore the importance of implementing "good practices" in service-learning. Those with LSAHE grants should be encouraged to build tight links between course content and service, hold in-class discussions about students' service experiences, and provide training and ongoing supervision.

Although the large majority of programs provided service in the areas of education and/or health, the survey results indicate that service in other settings was associated with more-positive benefits to students. Although more research is needed to confirm and explain this finding, it raises a reason for caution about the growing emphasis on college student service to K–12 institutions (e.g., the America Reads initiative, which promotes college students' involvement as tutors and mentors to elementary school children).

These results also raise questions about the benefits of course-based service. Given the modest gains for students, it is reasonable to question whether sufficient grounds exist to encourage course-based service-learning as opposed to other forms of service-learning or community service.

Directions for Future Research

Low response rates to RAND and UCLA surveys, reliance on self-reported outcomes, and other methodological problems such as self-selection indicate a strong need for further research about the impacts of participation in service-learning on student development. Longitudinal studies that compare students who are randomly assigned to service versus nonservice conditions, thereby controlling for self-selection, are especially needed.

In addition, studies that compare course-based service-learning to other forms of service will inform the question of whether course-based service-learning provides more value to students than does co-curricular service-learning or simple community service. This is especially important given the finding that course-based service was associated with fewer hours of service per student than was co-curricular service, thereby limiting benefits to communities.

More research on "good practices" is also needed. For example, a study that selects courses or programs that adhere to the highest standards of service-learning would indicate the potential for service-learning to enhance education if implemented properly. Our results provide some unexpected evidence of good practices that also should be further investigated, particularly the finding that students who volunteer in organizations that are not related to education or health report more-positive outcomes. Information regarding the optimal intensity (number of hours) of service is also needed.

INCREASING INSTITUTIONAL SUPPORT AND CAPACITY FOR SERVICE

Conclusions

LSAHE succeeded in increasing the number of opportunities for students to serve. The strategy of funding consortia was especially effective since it enabled a large number of institutions to participate in LSAHE. Between 1995 and 1997, almost one in eight higher education institutions nationwide participated in LSAHE.

Within institutions, LSAHE was particularly effective in boosting the number of service-learning courses offered by higher education institutions, with almost 3,000 new courses established, spanning a wide range of disciplines. Some participating institutions used their LSAHE grants to establish service centers, which coordinated a variety of service programs and facilitated student involvement in service. Others added service activities to new-student orientations or offered rewards and recognition for service participants.

The findings are more ambiguous with regard to the quality of students' service opportunities. Because institutions used their LSAHE grants to seed a variety of service initiatives throughout the campus, LSAHE-supported programs vary widely and are essentially indistinguishable from other service programs in higher education. If one accepts that course-based service-learning is better than other forms of service-learning (a question this evaluation did not address), the growth in service-learning courses would indicate that LSAHE improved the quality of service-learning in higher education. However, as described above, these courses appear to have only modest positive effects on student development.

It is still too early to determine whether institutions will be able to sustain their new courses and service opportunities after their LSAHE grants terminate. The evidence is mixed. On the one hand, the majority of programs are strongly dependent on temporary and grant money, with little or no permanent funding or staff. On the other hand, programs are able to replace some of their LSAHE grants with other funding, and the program directors themselves are optimistic about their ability to sustain their service programs.

Limitations or Barriers to Success

The evaluation identified a number of obstacles that must be overcome for higher education institutions with LSAHE grants to expand and sustain their service programs. From a national perspective, consortia were effective in increasing service opportunities for students by enabling more institutions to participate in LSAHE. However, the analysis of return on investment suggests some limits to this approach. Specifically, subgranting appears cost effective, but subsubgranting appears inefficient due to the high overhead costs of administering so many layers of funding.

At the institutional level, the most serious obstacle is faculty resistance to service-learning. Faculty are reluctant to invest the extra time that teaching service-learning courses entails, and many are skeptical of the educational value of service-learning. Institutions provide few incentives and many disincentives for faculty involvement in such courses and programs. This is a major barrier to increasing the number of service opportunities for students and also raises important questions about sustainability. Institutions with service centers were best positioned to overcome this resistance, since the centers could both recruit and support faculty.

Administrative disinterest is another barrier. Programs that have strong administrative advocates fare better than those that are left to their own devices. In some cases, charismatic leaders compensate for neglect at higher levels of the organization, but a lack of administrative support generally threatens program expansion and sustainability.

Programmatic Implications

In its relations with individual institutions, CNS now promotes sustainability in two ways: (a) grant amounts decline over successive years, providing institutions with opportunities to gradually decrease their financial dependence on LSAHE, and (b) institutions are required to match grant funds. Often, however, the matching funds are "in-kind" contributions that represent at best lukewarm commitments on the part of institutions toward service programs. A stronger matching fund requirement might improve the prospects for continuing programs after LSAHE funds expire.

It might also be useful for CNS to be more specific about the characteristics of "high quality" service programs. For example, CNS might consider encouraging programs to implement the good practices that contribute to high quality service programs, both course based and co-curricular.

Similarly, CNS might be more explicit about how institutions with LSAHE grants should seek to expand and enhance service programs. This would include developing service centers, promoting faculty involvement, directing attention to building strong community relations, and linking service programs to local values and traditions.

Finally, CNS might benefit from fine-tuning its approach to consortia, especially if future research indicates that subsubgranting is less cost effective than subgranting.

Directions for Future Research

The most important research needed in this area is follow-up research to determine whether institutions with LSAHE grants were able to sustain their service-learning courses and programs after their grants ended. Such research should also address the factors that affect sustainability. Additional research is needed to determine the return on investment for consortia that engage in subsubgranting.

This information will greatly enrich the analysis of return on investment. If institutions succeed in sustaining their LSAHE-supported programs, the benefits that communities derive from LSAHE grants over time will exceed—possibly by a large margin—the costs.

RECOMMENDATIONS

The evaluation results support the following five recommendations.

Clarify Goals of LSAHE

LSAHE would almost certainly show stronger results if CNS offered more-specific and focused goals. Grantees had little to guide them on how to balance service to communities, student learning, and institutional change. Although grantees valued the opportunity to design programs that suited the local context, the result for LSAHE nationally was a highly diffuse set of activities, with limited impact in any given area. With regard to community impacts, for example, services were provided across a wide array of settings rather than concentrated in areas where LSAHE as a whole could make a strong impact. Similarly, the small impact of service-learning on student development reflects in part the wide variety of learning goals and the lack of a shared operational definition of key concepts, such as "life skills" and "social responsibility." As CNS and the LSAHE program directors clarify their goals, they can design courses and programs that are tightly linked to desired outcomes.

Encourage More Direct Service

Community organizations assigned a very high value to the contributions of student volunteers, and LSAHE was successful in engaging students in meeting community needs. Yet even more could have been achieved had programs devoted more effort to direct service in relation to capacity building or other activities. In the future, programs should be encouraged to boost service to communities while maintaining quality. This approach will also have benefits for students, since volunteering for more than 20 hours was associated with more positive outcomes for students enrolled in service-learning courses.

Specify "Good Practices" in Service-Learning, and Hold Programs Accountable for Implementing Them

The RAND Student Survey indicates that the perceived effects of participation in service-learning differ as a function of course characteristics. Thus, CNS should encourage institutions to implement "good practices" in their course-based service-learning. These include linking the service experience to course content, discussing service in class, training and supervising student volunteers, and ensuring that students volunteer for more than 20 hours.

Ask More of Institutions

Although institutions were required to provide matching funds for LSAHE grants, in-kind contributions were accepted, as were other grant funds. Thus, LSAHE provided only limited incentives for institutions to increase their direct support for service-learning. To the extent possible, more should be asked of institutions as a means of building their commitment to and ability to sustain service programs.

Institutions should especially be asked to support the development of service centers where they do not already exist. These centers play a critical role in supporting faculty, coordinating community relations, recruiting and supervising students, and providing quality control and continuity. Institutions without centers face barriers to developing and sustaining service programs. Institutions should also be encouraged to support faculty involvement in service-learning and to reduce disincentives to participation. For example, institutions might seek to recognize faculty participation in service-learning in personnel (tenure and promotion) reviews or to provide release time or summer support to faculty interested in developing service-learning courses.

At the same time, CNS should strive to meet institutional needs. For example, a fourth year of funding may improve some institutions' abilities to institutionalize and sustain their service activities; others may benefit from postgrant follow-on activities, including technical assistance in fund-raising.

Continue LSAHE Pending Further Research

LSAHE provided seed money for service-learning at a time when higher education as a whole was experiencing severe financial constraints. With a stronger economy, most higher education institutions are faring better and hence may be better able to support new initiatives such as service-learning.

The benefits of LSAHE for service-learning went well beyond financial support, however. LSAHE increased the visibility of service-learning within higher education, provided an incentive for institutions to develop service programs, and sent a message about the perceived responsibilities of students and institutions. LSAHE also was a source of technical assistance and information about program design and implementation.

On the other hand, participation in LSAHE-supported courses offered only modest benefits to students. In addition, program costs exceeded the estimated value to communities over the three-year study period. We believe, however, that by implementing the recommendations provided here, LSAHE can substantially increase its effectiveness as both a pedagogical tool and a public investment.

Further research will inform decisionmaking about future directions for LSAHE. The three highest priorities for future research should be (1) continuing the study of student outcomes, including efforts to identify and measure the outcomes of "good practices"; (2) following up those grantees whose funding expired in 1996 or 1997 to determine the extent to which they have been able to sustain their programs; and (3) assessing the value and effects of institutional investments in capacity building.

REFERENCES

Astin, A. W., L. J. Sax, and J. Avalos (in press). Long-Term Effects of Volunteerism During the Undergraduate Years. *Review of Higher Education.*

Barber, B. (1992). *An Aristocracy of Everyone: The Politics of Education and the Future of America.* New York: Oxford University Press.

Berman, P., and M. W. McLaughlin (1978). *Federal Programs Supporting Educational Change: Vol. VIII, Implementing and Sustaining Innovations.* Santa Monica: RAND, R-1589/8-HEW.

The Boyer Commission on Educating Undergraduates in the Research University (1998). *Reinventing Undergraduate Education: A Blueprint for America's Research Universities.* Stony Brook: State University of New York. http://notes.cc.sunysb.edu/Pres/boyer.ns

Cohen, J., and D. Kinsey (1994). Doing Good and Scholarship: A Service-Learning Study. *Journalism Educator*, Winter, 4-14.

Corporation for National and Community Service (1994). *Learn and Serve America, Higher Education Program Summary.* Washington, DC: CNS.

Council for Aid to Education (1997). Breaking the Social Contract: The Fiscal Crisis in Higher Education. Santa Monica: RAND, CAE-100(5/97).

Eyler, J., D. Giles, and T. Braxton (1997). The Impact of Service-Learning on College Students. *Michigan Journal of Community Service Learning, 4,* 5-15.

Giles, D. E., E. P. Honnet, and S. Migliore (1991). *Research Agenda for Combining Service and Learning in the 1990s.* Raleigh, NC: National Society for Experiential Education.

Greene, D., and G. Diehm (1995). Educational and Service Outcomes of a Service Integration Effort. *Michigan Journal of Community Service Learning, 2,* 54-62.

Kupiec, T. (1993). *Rethinking Tradition: Integrating Service With Academic Study on College Campuses.* Providence: The Education Commission of the States, Campus Compact.

Markus, G., J. Howard, and D. King (1993). Integrating Community Service and Classroom Instruction Enhances Learning: Results from an Experiment. *Educational Evaluation and Policy Analysis, 15,* 410-419.

Ostrow, J. (1995). Self-Consciousness and Social Position: On College Students Changing Their Minds About the Homeless. *Qualitative Sociology, 18,* 357-375.

Rhoads, R. (1998). In the Service of Citizenship: A Study of Student Involvement in Community Service. *The Journal of Higher Education, 69,* 277-297.

Sax, L. J., A. W. Astin, and H. S. Astin (1996). In Gray et al., *Evaluation of Learn and Serve America, Higher Education: First Year Report,* Vols. I and II. Santa Monica: RAND, PM-528.

Study Group on the Conditions of Excellence in American Higher Education (1984). *Involvement in Learning: Realizing the Potential of American Higher Education.* Washington, DC: National Institute of Education.

Tice, C. (1994). Forging University-Community Collaboration: The Agency Perspective on National Service. *Michigan Journal of Community Service Learning, 1*, 21-28.

Wingspread Group on Higher Education (1993). *An American Imperative: Higher Expectations for Higher Education: An Open Letter to Those Concerned About the American Future.* Racine, WI: The Johnson Foundation.